HAVANA

BY THE SAME AUTHOR

The White Man in the Tree and
Other Stories

CHILDREN/YOUNG ADULT
•
Frozen in Time: Clarence
Birdseye's Outrageous Idea about
Frozen Food

Battle Fatigue

World without Fish

The Story of Salt

The Girl Who Swam to Euskadi

The Cod's Tale

HAVANA

A SUBTROPICAL DELIRIUM

MARK KURLANSKY

BLOOMSBURY

NEW YORK · LONDON · OXFORD · NEW DELHI · SYDNEY

Bloomsbury USA
An imprint of Bloomsbury Publishing Plc

1385 Broadway	50 Bedford Square
New York	London
NY 10018	WC1B 3DP
USA	UK

www.bloomsbury.com

BLOOMSBURY and the Diana logo are trademarks of Bloomsbury Publishing Plc

First published 2017
This paperback edition 2018

Sketches on pages 18, 24, 40, 50, 62, 73, 86, 158, 181, 192, 210, 220, 229
© Mark Kurlansky

Excerpt from *Cuba Libre* copyright © 1948 by Langston Hughes and
Ben Frederick Carruthers. Copyright renewed 1976 by George
Houston Bass, executor of Langston Hughes. By permission of
Harold Ober Associates Incorporated.

ISBN: HB: 978-1-63286-391-1
PB: 978-1-63286-392-8
EPUB: 978-1-63286-393-5

Library of Congress cataloging-in-publication data is available.

4 6 8 10 9 7 5 3

Typeset by Newgen Knowledge Works (P) Ltd., Chennai, India.
Printed and bound in the U.S.A. by Berryville Graphics Inc.,
Berryville, Virginia

To find out more about our authors and books visit
www.bloomsbury.com. Here you will find extracts, author interviews,
details of forthcoming events, and the option to sign up for
our newsletters.

Bloomsbury books may be purchased for business or promotional
use. For information on bulk purchases please contact Macmillan
Corporate and Premium Sales Department at
specialmarkets@macmillan.com.

*To Cuban writers, the ones who supported the Revolution,
the ones who opposed it, and the ones who did both.*

*Esta especie de ensoñacíon o desvario subtropical, bajo el
sol, al borde de la bahía hermosa, diabólicamente hermosa,
abierta a las peligrosas aguas del golfo de México, atestadas
de tiburones y de almas en pena.*

This subtropical delirium, under the sun, by the edge
of a beautiful bay, diabolically beautiful, open to the
perilous waters of the Gulf of Mexico, swarming with
sharks and lost souls.

— ABILIO ESTÉVEZ, *Los Palacios Distantes* (2002)

BIRD'S-EYE VIEW OF HAVANA, CUBA.

Habana Vieja seen from the sea, from Illustrated News, July 23, 1853

CONTENTS

A Black-and-White Feast

El corazón es un loco
que no sabe de un color.

The heart is a fool
that knows no color.

— JOSÉ MARTÍ, *Versos Sencillos* (1891)

F I WERE EVER to make an old-fashioned film noir—with a cynical plot full of intrigue, violence, and sudden twists, filmed on dark and menacing streets in misty black and white—I would shoot it in Havana.

My reason for choosing to shoot in black and white might not be immediately apparent to people who know Havana. Havana is a Caribbean city with yellow and pink and turquoise buildings set against a hot cerulean sky and a sea that is bright blue with a dark cobalt stripe formed by the Gulf Stream, always present in the distance.

Sometimes, as Americans in particular have occasionally observed, the sea off of Havana can appear violet when it reflects the sky moments before daybreak. Ernest Hemingway, for whom "violet" would have been too flowery a word, described the Gulf Stream there as "nearly purple." But Habaneros—that is, the people of Havana—tend to be less poetic about the sea, and the only one I ever found who thought the waters of Havana were violet was the mid-twentieth-century Habanero poet and novelist José Lezama Lima, who wrote:

The violet sea longs for the birth of gods,
For to be born here is an unspeakable feast . . .

John Muir, the Scot who became America's great naturalist and perhaps first environmentalist, went to Cuba in 1868, the same year he first saw and made famous Yosemite. To Muir, Havana was a yellow city: "On one side of the harbor was a city of these yellow plants; on the other, a city of yellow stucco houses, narrowly and confusedly congregated." Muir found yellow everywhere. The hill on which the Morro Castle guards the opening of the harbor, according to Muir, was covered with yellow weeds.

Similarly, British novelist Anthony Trollope, on his 1859 visit, called Havana "the dingy yellow town." And that is how American Impressionist Childe Hassam painted it. Although he was a great colorist in New York, New England, and France, when he went to Havana in 1895, he painted yellow buildings faded to pastel by the white-hot sunlight—a dingy yellow town. In his paintings of Havana, even the shadows were muted—into a pastel blue—and the only true saturated colors were the red and gold of the Spanish flags. Hassam loved flags.

Contemporary Cuban writer Pedro Juan Gutiérrez, who consciously avoids lyrical flourishes, made an exception for Havana at sunset, which he called "the beautiful golden city in the dusk," and it is true that when the sun's rays burn into the city at an angle almost parallel to the ground, Havana is a golden city.

Federico García Lorca, the great Spanish poet, is beloved in Havana for his boyish charm and because he came to a tragic end—he was shot by Fascists at the outbreak of the Spanish Civil War. Tragic endings always play well in Havana. But in 1930 he wrote, "Havana has the yellow of Cádiz, the pink of Seville turning carmine and the green of Granada, with the slight phosphorescence of fish."

Were these writers seeing the same city that I was seeing?

•

ONE REASON FOR the difference between these writers' impressions, at least in the early accounts, and mine was that these writers first saw Havana from the sea.

Havana is located on the north coast of Cuba, along a primary shipping lane that runs between North America and Europe, and through the Caribbean to Mexico and South America. It and San Juan, Puerto Rico, which is situated much farther from North America and Mexico, are the only major Caribbean ports on the Atlantic Ocean. Most Caribbean ports are on the Caribbean side of their respective islands, where ships have to struggle through treacherous inter-island passages to get to the Atlantic.

The French knew the right place for a port, establishing the capital of what is now Haiti in Cap-Haïtien, on the Atlantic coast, but after the Haitian Revolution of 1791–1804, Port-au-Prince, on the Caribbean coast, became the capital. In Cuba, on the other hand, the Spanish originally did it wrong, establishing the island's capital at Santiago, on the Caribbean side, and only later moving it to Havana, on the Atlantic coast. Havana has a perfect harbor, with a long, narrow inlet leading to the long, wide, and well sheltered Havana Bay.

That bay and its waterfront in the old part of Havana, now called Habana Vieja, was once the heart of the city, the place where every visitor first disembarked, where huge warehouses of the nation's ample sugar and tobacco crops were loaded and shipped abroad, where goods entered and were inspected by customs officials.

In *To Have and Have Not*, Hemingway's only book set in Havana, published in 1937, the action takes place on the waterfront of Habana Vieja's eastern side, with docks and warehouses, stevedores and rough bars and cafés. At that time, the waterfront was populated by the poor looking for work, the "street bums" sleeping against the walls, seamen and gangsters and their murderous henchmen.

Tourists visiting the restored colonial sites in Habana Vieja today only have to turn right and walk a block or two to reach this once famous area. But almost no one does.

Most tourists have little sense that there is a waterfront and a harbor in the neighborhood. The bums and the gangsters and most of the seamen are also gone.

Today, people arrive by airplane, which offers a completely different view of Havana than arriving by boat. You fly in low over vast, green, and well-trimmed farms outside the city. The taxi rides a bumpy road past a few not very tall high-rises, unusual in Havana, including a large state psychiatric clinic, and drab gray buildings, or rust-streaked, turquoise, and rotting pink ones—resembling birthday cakes left out too long. In surprisingly little time you are swiftly careening—if you have a younger, healthier taxi—around the curves of the oceanfront road, the Malecón, and into Central Havana, reaching it so quickly it is hard to believe that this is a city of two million people.

From much of the city, the ocean is visible, blue and empty. Seldom is a boat of any kind seen—certainly not recreational boats, but not even fishing boats. This seems unnatural, because it is obvious that there are fish out there. The dark streak of the fish-rich Gulf Stream, the great marlin grounds that drew Hemingway, is visible from the shore. Men and boys stand along the seawall fishing. Sometimes they float out on an inner tube to access larger catch. The prize is *pargo*, the large local snapper. Hemingway called the *pargo* by an American name, muttonfish, and said it could be caught on the rocks off the Morro, the castle guarding the harbor. Locals catch them using minnows or squid that they net. But there are many other Caribbean species as well, most reef-feeding fish, and many with folkloric names like *pez perro*, the dogface, a goofy-looking bucktoothed creature.

But nothing is being caught from boats. Even in adjacent Cojímar, Havana's "fishing village," there are no boats in sight, and the few remaining fishermen are elderly, no longer fishing but loaded with reminiscences, sometimes of fishing with Hemingway. Explanations for this lack of boats range from a fuel shortage to the theory that all working boats have left for Florida. And the real reason probably does have something to do with the city's proximity to Florida, because there is still an active fishing fleet on the southern coast of Cuba, though there it is focused on lobster and shellfish.

Since the 1959 Cuban Revolution and the subsequent 1960 U.S. trade embargo, there has been little marine traffic in and out of Havana. Even during the years of Cuba's close ties to the Soviet Union, when there were regular shipments arriving from Eastern Europe, there was never enough activity to create the old-time bustle.

In fact, Havana Bay became a dank, foul place, and until the mid-1980s, when Cuba got United Nations money to clean up the harbor, a tremendous amount of sewage from rivers and storm drains flowed into its waters. Slaughterhouses, a yeast factory, two alcohol distilleries, a leather tannery, and the flaming oil refinery in Regla, on the eastern side of the waterfront, contributed to the pollution. Three decades of cleanup work in Havana Bay has not increased its usage, either. In fact, since the demise of the Soviet Union in 1991, the harbor has been used even less.

This could be changing. Immediately after President Barack Obama announced a thawing of relations with Cuba in 2015, American entrepreneurs started laying plans for boat service to Havana, even though the trade embargo was still in place. But the old harbor and waterfront are not likely to ever again be what they once were. If the harbor does become lively again, it will most likely be as a tourist port rather than a commercial one.

The truth is that what was once the most perfect harbor in the Caribbean, the one that first inspired Havana to be built, is now a bit dated. In the days of smaller ships, the harbor, with its deep water and narrow entrance—only about three hundred yards wide for almost half a mile, until it broadens to several square miles of sheltered water—offered a great military advantage, both for defense and offense. An attacker trying to bottle up a fleet could sink a ship at the harbor's entrance, closing it for entry or exit. The harbor is still an ideal shelter for sitting out a hurricane, but it is not deep enough for modern shipping, and a larger deepwater harbor is now being built to the west of the city. In the old harbor, the entrance is too narrow. In addition, although Regla is still a serviceable location for shipping to and from eastern Cuba, the streets on the Habana Vieja side are too narrow for moving goods by truck.

•

THAT DENSE, CROWDED world of narrow spaces in Habana Vieja is where my film noir could take place. The light there is so hot it is white, and that makes the shadows very dark. This tropical city was built to have as much shade as possible, and the narrow streets are mostly dark. In fact, in Habana Vieja, the streets are so narrow that until recent times, awnings were strung between the buildings on either side to keep the street below shaded.

But there are other reasons for seeing Havana in black and white. Because of the U.S. embargo, color film and color film processing have not been available, so for many years

Awnings across the buildings on O'Reilly Street in Habana Vieja provide shade for shoppers, 1871.

after the revolution, the country's leading photographers, such as Raúl Corrales and Alberto Korda, shot in black and white. (A true Habanero, Korda, famous for his black-and-white portrait of Che Guevara, said that he had become a photographer "to meet women.")

One of the best Havana novels reads like a film noir. You don't think in color while reading *El Acoso* (*The Chase*), by Alejo Carpentier. It is a testament to the openness of Habaneros to foreigners that Carpentier—who was born in Switzerland to a French father and a Russian mother, died in Paris, and had a French accent when he spoke Spanish—is accepted in the city as a great Habanero. Most Habaneros do not even realize that he was not born there.

The Chase is set in the 1950s, during the dictatorship of Fulgencio Batista, and is the story of a political activist being pursued through Havana by secret police agents. It is one of several Carpentier novels that influenced Colombian Gabriel García Márquez and other Latin American writers to turn to what came to be called "magical realism." But despite the book's magical quality, it is full of gritty realism because it is set in the streets of Havana. It captures what the city looks like, feels like, and especially smells like. There are occasional references to color, though: "Following the paint smeared on the houses, he moved, he moved from ocher to ash, from green to mulberry, passing from the portal with a broken coat of arms over it to the portal adorned with filthy cornucopias." And that has always been Havana—ornate but disheveled, somewhat like an unshaven man in a tattered tuxedo.

Perhaps it is the book's story line that so suggests a film noir, or the fact that it takes place mostly at night, making it seem like a chase through a black-and-white city. Carpentier hit on the true essence of Havana when he wrote, in his 1970 book *La Ciudad de las Columnas* (*The City of Columns*), "The old city . . . is a city of shadows, made by using shadows." Havana was built by Europeans looking for shade in a hot country; they created a shadowy world.

In *The Chase*, darkness heightens the sense of smell. For, like all tropical cities, Havana is filled with sweet, sour, and bitter scents, many of them unpleasant. It would help if the garbage were picked up more often, but there are many other smells as well. Carpentier wrote of "the stink of the kitchens of the poor." He even wrote of "the scent of termite-eaten papers." Hunt through old used books with slightly eaten pages at the stalls in the Plaza de Armas, the city's oldest square, and you will know that scent.

No one could write about a city with as much detail as Carpentier does without loving it for all its stench. As Nelson Algren once wrote about Chicago, "Before you earn the right to rap any sort of joint, you have to love it a little while." *The Chase* was Carpentier's homage to the dark and rough city.

Another enduring black-and-white image of Havana comes from the photographs of Walker Evans. Carpentier even makes a reference to one of them in *The Chase*. In 1932 or 1933, Evans went down to Cuba with a commission to illustrate a book, which was never published, called "The Crime of Cuba." But in three weeks of shooting, and also a lot of drinking with Hemingway at the Hotel Ambos Mundos, Papa treating, Evans shot his black-and-white Havana masterpieces. His pictures do not show the Depression-era poverty of his American pictures, just streets full of people trying to look all right in a hopelessly tattered world.

There have also been real film noirs of the city, such as the 1959 Carol Reed black-and-white adaptation of the 1958 novel *Our Man in Havana*. The fact that the book's author, Graham Greene, also wrote the screenplay makes this one of the rare movies that lives up to the novel on which it was based.

The story is one of a British vacuum cleaner salesman who convinces British intelligence that vacuum cleaner drawings are designs for a weapons system in the Cuban mountains. His plan is to get the British to pay him so he can send his daughter to prep school in Switzerland. It could be argued that the story is too comic to be a film noir. Fidel Castro, who permitted the film's crew to shoot in Havana, complained that it made too much light of Batista's security operatives. But the story does have a dark side, including a torturing police agent with a cigarette case made of human skin and scenes of people being shot down in the street—dramatic flashes of gunshots in the dark.

Greene's book is fundamentally a comedy, but, as the novel states, "someone always leaves a banana skin on the scene of a tragedy."

He had originally set his story in 1938 Estonia but realized that the Nazi occupation there was perhaps too dark a setting for an espionage comedy. He later decided that in "fantastic Havana," a comedy could be set in the midst of "the absurdities of the cold war." He reasoned, "For who can accept the survival of Western capitalism as a great cause?" But as Castro pointed out, if you were Cuban, Batista's dictatorship wasn't very funny. A murderous kleptocracy in close partnership with American organized crime, it was marked by both wretched poverty and glittering wealth. Foreigners remember the Havana of that time as a kind of romantic brothel where beautiful people dressed elegantly and listened to great music in famous nightclubs. But Habaneros remember it as a place of terror where innocent, even heroic, people were beaten, dragged through the streets, and murdered in daylight and at night.

In truth, Havana, a city long famous for "fun," is laced with reminders of a tragic and impassioned history. On the city streets in various neighborhoods are plaques marking spots where Batista's victims were cut down. There are the places that used to have barracoons, where slaves were warehoused and put on display for the amusement of the rich as late as the 1870s. One barracoon stood on the edge of Habana Vieja, and another on what was once the western edge of town but is now the central neighborhood of Vedado. By the picturesque stoneworks near the mouth of the port once stood military-run centers where owners could take their slaves to be beaten or mutilated by experts while unfazed passersby heard them scream. Near the western barracoon, a plaque marks the quarry where in 1869 José Martí, the central hero of Cuban history, labored on a chain gang as a teenage Spanish political prisoner. Released to exile in Spain, he wrote in a letter to the Spanish people: "Infinite pain: for the pain of imprisonment is the harshest, most devastating pain, murdering the mind, searing the soul, leaving marks that will never be erased."

CHAIN-GANG IN THE CATHEDRAL PLAZA, HAVANA.—From a Sketch by our Special Artist.—[See Page 1226.]

A chain gang on the Plaza de la Catedral in the epoch of Martí's servitude. Harper's Weekly, *December 3, 1871.*

Below the Morro are the sixteenth-century fortifications of La Cabaña, a favorite tourist spot, where Che Guevara—a man with the looks of a cinema hero—held his tribunals and executed so many people by firing squad that Castro removed him from his post and made him the country's bank president instead. On the other side of the harbor opening stands La Punta, where in 1852 the rebel Narciso López was publicly garroted.

In Havana every splash of light has its dark spot.

•

HAVANA IS HOT, and dealing with heat is a central part of living there. "The heat is a malign plague invading everything," wrote Leonardo Padura Fuentes in the opening of his contemporary murder mystery *Máscaras* (titled *Havana Red* in English). "The heat descends like a tight, stretchy cloak of red silk, wrapping itself around bodies, trees and things, to inject there the dark poison of despair and a slower, certain death." The book's central character, the police lieutenant Mario Conde, asks, *"¿Pero cómo puede hacer tanto calor, coño?"* It is the eternal Havana question: How can it be so fucking hot?

In December, cooler air comes in by sea from Florida, kicking up the surf and making it foam across the Malecón. In January and February the temperature drops to a very pleasant seventy-five degrees, and some think that this is the best time to visit. But if you are not experiencing heat, you are not really experiencing Havana.

Habaneros have developed an expertise about which streets to walk on and stick to the ones that line up with the coast to afford a sea breeze. Shade is found everywhere; Habaneros are never seen sunning themselves if they can help it. They glisten with sweat, which is why they are also known for frequent bathing.

Havana is not a city for people who are squeamish about sweat. Sweat is one of the many defining smells in redolent Havana and is a leitmotif in almost all Havana literature. They sweat in all of Padura's mystery novels. They sweat in Cirilo Villaverde's great nineteenth-century classic novel *Cecilia Valdés*.

Sweat was a precept of classlessness in a city heavily demarcated by classes—everybody sweats. In *The Chase*, where sweat is almost one of the central characters, Carpentier described wealthy well-dressed women at a theater: "The furs they wore in spite of the heat made moisture collect on their necks and bosoms." Rich people just sweat in better clothes.

•

MOST OF THE central figures of Havana culture have experienced either forced or self-imposed exile at some time in their lives. And the Habaneros who leave rarely lose an excruciating nostalgia for their city, because it is not like any other place.

People seem to irrecoverably fall under Havana's spell. No one visits the city—let alone lives there—and forgets it. Cuba has a history that is unlike any other country's, certainly unlike any other Spanish colony's, and Havana's history and culture stand apart from the rest of Cuba's.

People in Havana find it difficult to imagine the rest of the island, let alone the rest of the world—an attitude most New Yorkers and Parisians can understand. Life is not real outside the city.

Though Cuba is an island, people in Havana tend to see their city as an island within the island. And actually, it almost was. Until the nineteenth century, Havana was a walled city on the tip of a seaside peninsula that juts into Havana Bay with water on three sides and a nearly straight wall on the fourth. The wall ran from the opening of the harbor straight along the western edge of the old city to the bay on the other side. The walled side was the only land connection, and in the seventeenth century the colonial government proposed digging a moat along the wall, which would have made Havana literally an island.

But it wasn't necessary. Starting in the eighteenth century, at nine o'clock at night at the fortifications of La Cabaña, a cannon was fired and the gates were closed. You could stay out all night in Havana. Many did. But once the cannon fired, no one could enter or leave the city until morning. Today there is no more wall, no more gates, but the cannon at the harbor entrance is still fired at nine o'clock every night by a contingent of soldiers in eighteenth-century uniforms, accompanied by a drum roll, to remind people of how insular life in the capital still is.

Havana's isolation was seldom viewed as something positive. For Dulce María Loynaz, a leading twentieth-century Havana poet, *isla* was always a word that implied loneliness:

> *Surrounded everywhere by the sea*
> *I am an island clinging to the wind's stem.*
> *It doesn't matter if I scream or pray,*
> *Nobody hears me.*

"Nadie escucha mi voz si rezo o grito." Nobody hears my voice whether I scream or pray. Perhaps this is why, throughout their tortured history, Habaneros have always screamed and prayed so loudly. On an island on an island, it takes a lot to be heard.

And yet—and perhaps with the same perversity with which moviegoers find film noir romantic, even though they are sad stories of luckless people—Havana, for all its smells, sweat, crumbling walls, isolation, and difficult history, is the most romantic city in the world. Endless love songs have been written about it. The city always beguiles.

ONE

Change

✺⦚✦⦙✺

Todo el mundo tiene una ciudad distinta en la cabeza.

Everybody has a different city in his head.

— EDMUNDO DESNOES ON HAVANA,
in *Inconsolable Memories*, 1965

THERE IS A GREAT deal of disagreement about Havana, partly because in Havana disagreeing is a way of life. But most everyone agrees that it is like no other city on earth. How did Havana become so different (though not as different as Columbus thought when he reported that there was a place called Avan, where "the inhabitants are born with tails")?

Historians point to one uprising or another revolt that shaped the city but in truth it is change itself that has given Havana its character. It has had a history of upheaval and change like no other place. Change is one of the fundamental conditions here.

To start with, Havana was founded three times in three different places.

After Christopher Columbus in 1492 declared the island of Cuba "the most beautiful that eyes have ever seen," he sent an emissary to talk to the locals, who he thought were

Chinese. Columbus didn't have anyone with him who actually spoke Chinese, so he sent someone who spoke Arabic, reasoning that he was at least some kind of Asianist. There is some evidence that Columbus knew that he was not in Asia but it is not clear why he thought an Arab speaker might be helpful.

Not much is known of the original inhabitants of the area, the Tainos. Once Columbus acknowledged that they weren't Chinese, he noted in his diary that they seemed to be "good people" and would make excellent servants. He kidnapped a few to bring back to his sponsors in Spain.

In 1511, the Spanish sent Diego Velázquez de Cuéllar to Cuba with three hundred men for what the Spanish called conquest and what today is called genocide. Few Tainos survived. According to legend, the Taino leader, Hatuey, later honored in Havana by a popular brand of beer, was strapped to a pole on a pile of wood for burning. Threatened with painful death, he refused to reveal where the island's gold was, most probably because there was none. Then the Spanish offered him a cross and told him that if he accepted the Christian God, he would go to heaven. According to the story, Hatuey asked if Christians went to heaven and the Spanish assured him that they did. Hatuey's last words before they lit the fire were "If Christians go to heaven, I do not want to go."

One reason for speculation that this often-repeated story is not true is that it so clearly resembles Habanero humor. Habaneros love stories that are told at the expense of people in charge, always starting with a soft, anecdotal setup and ending with a biting short punch line. The Hatuey story is like the popular "Pepito" jokes of Cuba today, which are usually about Fidel Castro, commonly referred to as "Fidel." Indeed, the story may be the founding Pepito joke. A more recent example:

When Castro was trying to prevent Havana from becoming overcrowded, he proposed moving new arrivals from Oriente Province back to where they had come from. Pepito suggested to him that they provide three hundred buses and a Mercedes.

"What is the Mercedes for?" Castro asked.

"You, Comandante." (Castro himself was from Oriente.)

ON JULY 25, 1514, Velázquez sent forth one of his lieutenants, Pánfilo de Narváez, to found a town to be called San Cristóbal, since they were setting out on San Cristóbal Day. According to Bartolomé de Las Casas (remembered today as the conquistador who documented the genocide of the Tainos), Pánfilo was a very large, redheaded man who was not only exceptionally brutal, even for that crowd, but also unusually stupid. So the evidence is that Havana was founded by a moronic thug.

Pánfilo chose to build the town on a western inlet on the island's southern (Caribbean) coast. He was apparently not a good enough sailor—he was eventually lost at sea on an expedition to Florida—to realize that the more desirable location was the northern coast on the Atlantic. He named the settlement San Cristóbal de la Habana, and no one seems to know where the "Habana" came from. It is thought that the Taino chief of the region was named Habaguanex, but why would Pánfilo name a new town after the chief of the people he was killing? Some believe the place he chose was the spot that Columbus called Avan, but only because of the vague similarity in names and the fact that Columbus said Avan was located in the western part of the island. Today the port there is called Batabonó, and it is a small village of little distinction aside from being where Hernán Cortés outfitted his original expedition to Mexico.

Not only was San Cristóbal de la Habana founded on the wrong coast, but it was also situated near an unbearable mosquito-infested, disease-plagued swamp. Settlers endured a harsh existence there for a few years and then moved directly north some thirty miles across what was by chance the narrowest part of the island—to the right coast, where they found another buggy area. There they founded the new San Cristóbal de la Habana at the mouth of a river that the Tainos called Casiguagua but that today is known as the Almendares. The river runs through residential sections of present-day Havana, dividing the once-fashionable neighborhood of Vedado from the newer, also once-fashionable neighborhood of Miramar. The river had good freshwater and has long served as a water supply for

Havana, but aside from that it is unclear why the settlers chose this spot, since it was only a short distance from a superbly sheltered bay with more comfortable and defensible high ground. That spot was known as the Puerto de Carenas because it was used for careening, the term for hauling ships onto dry dock and caulking their hulls with pitch, which was found along the rocky shore.

In San Cristóbal de la Habana II, the settlers were again plagued by insects and disease, and finally in 1519 they relocated to the hill overlooking the bay at Puerto de Carenas, on the spot that is currently the Plaza de Armas, Havana's oldest square. They had finally learned that if you live by the water, you will live a lot better on high ground than low ground. The official founding date of San Cristóbal de la Habana III is November 16, 1519, not because anything in particular happened on that day, but because the pope had switched San Cristóbal Day from July 25 to November 16. According to legend, the colonists observed a mass under a large ceiba, or silk-cotton tree. Then they dropped the saint from the name.

•

THE FIRST HOUSES in this third Havana were temporary mud-walled, thatch-roofed, dirt-floored huts facing the sea. The bay was soon filled with galleons loaded with booty brought in from Mexico and the Americas, to be shipped to Spain. For all the wealth passing through it, however, Havana was not a town of luxuries. There were so many tortoises and crabs crawling through the young town that after dark a tremendous racket of clawing and shuffling was reportedly heard, a gnawing noise that was the sound of Havana at night. In 1655, an English pirate ship sent a raiding party into town, but upon hearing in the dark what sounded like the scuffling of a huge army, they retreated to their ship. They had been pushed back by an army of tortoises.

The early Habaneros killed the tortoises, cut them into strips, and dried them into tasajo, by all accounts an unappealing dish, which could be reconstituted in boiling water for sailors on voyages back to Spain. Apparently, too, drying tortoise has an unpleasant smell, or perhaps the rotting leftover parts do, because eventually, due to the odor, the town government banned tasajo making within the town limits.

But that was an early Havana. There have been many since.

TWO

The Hated Sea

Odio el mar, sólo hermoso cuando gime.

I hate the sea, beautiful only when it howls.

— JOSÉ MARTÍ, "Odio el Mar" (1882)

To the visitor, one of the great charms of Havana has always been that it is a strip of city facing a sparkling tropical sea, with the dark stripe of the Gulf Stream against the horizon. Hemingway was not the only foreigner for whom the sea was Havana's central attraction. But the people of Havana have not always felt that way.

To the east of the city is Varadero, one of the most beautiful beaches in the Americas. With more than fifty hotels, it is said to be the largest beach resort in the Caribbean. When I went to Cuba as a reporter in the 1980s and '90s, the Cuban official who took charge of my program, commonly referred to as a "handler," would always try to convince me to spend a few days of my brief working trip at Varadero. I went for a quick look, but never stayed, because there were no Cubans there. It was a place for Canadians and—depending on the epoch—either Eastern Europeans or Western Europeans. The *Lonely Planet* guidebook calls Varadero "the vanguard of Cuba's most important industry—tourism."

But Varadero holds little fascination for Habaneros. Aside from the few elite who used to vacation on the beach in what is now the western neighborhood of Miramar, beyond the Almendares River, the people of Havana have little affection for the sea.

Contemporary novelist Abilio Estévez wrote, "In Havana, I was always afraid of the sea. And since all roads in Havana lead to the sea, almost every road led me to fear."

Heberto Padilla, known for his 1984 autobiographical novel *Heroes Are Grazing in My Garden*, wrote:

If there is a landscape that truly repels me, it is the one on the cover of the first Spanish edition of *Heroes Are Grazing in My Garden*—you see a dreamy beach with palm trees and a deluxe sun, a scene from a tourist's postcard to be sent back home, stimulation directed at an attraction felt by Northerners, which I cannot bear.

And an aversion to the sea is not new for Habaneros. In "Odio el Mar" ("I Hate the Sea"), the great nineteenth-century poet José Martí wrote, "I hate the sea, enormous corpse, sad corpse where hateful creatures dwell."

Martí was born to poor Spanish immigrants living in a small house on the edge of Habana Vieja. Though always an Habanero in his heart and mind, he only lived the first sixteen years of his life there. A child prodigy who took up

painting and writing at an early age, he was a published
and known poet by the age of sixteen. He was also a passionate supporter of the movement to free Cuba from
Spanish control, and at age sixteen he started publishing a
newspaper called *La Patria Libre* dedicated to the cause of
Cuban independence, for which he was arrested and eventually exiled.

Martí, like many Habaneros before and after him, was a
wistful exile. To Habaneros, the struggle has always been
to stay home. Not going into exile, not leaving, remaining
in this special place is a triumph—albeit a triumph tinged
with sorrow. Every day, Habaneros pass the deserted
rooms, apartments, and houses of friends and loved ones
who have gone across the sea, "and you are left lonelier
and more lost than a shipwreck in the middle of the Gulf
Stream," as Pedro Juan Gutiérrez, the chronicler of contemporary Havana, wrote. And so, even proud Habaneros
stare across the sea, thinking of someone who crossed it.

This, in fact, is the most widely recognized symbol of
Havana. Giraldilla is a metal figure on top of the tower
of the Castillo de la Real Fuerza, which guards the seaward entrance to Habana Vieja. Actually, it's a copy, and
the real one is preserved in a museum in the nearby Plaza
de Armas, although even this 1634 statue appears to be a
copy of one in Sevilla.

According to legend, the statue represents Inés de
Bobadilla, Havana's only female ruler. She took over for
her husband, Hernando de Soto, after he left to explore

Florida. Never receiving word of his death, she stared out at the sea for years, looking for the ship on which he would return. It is perfect not only that the symbol of this city, celebrated for women, would be a woman, but also one who stares morosely across the sea to Florida, looking for a vanished love one.

That sense of loss is true of all the great Caribbean cities. But in Havana there is also the fear of arrivals. At the end of "Odio el Mar," Martí explains that the greater issue is not those who left, but those who came. He wrote:

> *I hate the sea, which without anger bears*
> *On its complacent back the ship*
> *That with music and flowers brings a tyrant.*

Havana's misfortunes have always come from the sea.

•

FOR ITS FIRST two centuries, Havana's central problem was that most of the time it was sitting on huge quantities of Spanish treasures. The Caribbean was the sea of pirates and privateers, who were working for foreign governments, enticed by the gold and other precious materials that the Spanish were taking from Mexico and South America, storing in Havana, and then shipping off to Sevilla. In 1503, the treasure that was brought to Spain, most of it offloaded in Havana, was valued at eight thousand Spanish gold coins, known at the time as ducados.

The quantity and value of the loot increased every year, so that in 1518 the treasure shipped from Havana to Spain was worth 120,000 ducados. Spanish galleons, which were huge ships for the time, were filling Havana Bay, lined with docks for storing and on- and off-loading all this treasure within eyesight of the small rustic town and its largely poor population. It was like wearing flashy jewelry in a bad neighborhood.

The sailors moving the valuables were a regular presence in this village and had a lasting impact. There was money to be made from sailors, and Havana became, and remained for centuries, notable for its bars and drinking spots, for gambling and prostitution.

In the sixteenth century, Havana had fewer than three hundred inhabitants and a few narrow streets of wooden houses, sometimes decorated with tile. The streets had prosaic, pragmatic names, which are still in use today. Some were named after their functions: The one where merchants set up shop was named Calle Mercaderes. Calle Basurero—Garbage Dump Street—no doubt not a popular street then, has happily lost its function and its name and is now Calle Teniente Rey, named after an army lieutenant. The first paved street—with cobblestones—was called Calle Empedrado, which means "paved street." Calle Aguacate was named for the large avocado tree that grew there. On Calle Damas, young women, *las damas*, used to hang out in the balconies, and an official of the Inquisition lived on Calle Inquisidor. Calle Obispo—Bishop Street—was the favorite walking route of Bishop Pedro Morell de Santa Cruz in the mid-sixteenth century. And a resident kept a lamp burning twenty-four hours a day to honor saints on Calle Lamparilla.

The sailors who came into Havana told tales of ruthless pirates who robbed, burned, and killed, and the townspeople shuddered in fear every time an unfamiliar ship appeared off the coast. Actually, some of these same sailors were themselves pirates, making note of the town's layout and defenses and where treasure was stored.

In 1538, an unidentified ship sailed into the harbor; its sailors spoke French, not Spanish. Hearing French chatter on the streets, the Habaneros locked themselves in their houses. The sailors were indeed French pirates, who soon set fire to a few of the houses. Wooden buildings with palm-frond roofs burn quickly. The townspeople, realizing that the pirates could easily burn down the entire town, scraped together six hundred ducados, which seemed to satisfy the Frenchmen, and they left.

Soon after, three Spanish ships arrived, and the Habaneros insisted that they pursue the French pirates. The Spaniards found them in an inlet not far away. But the first Spanish ship inadvertently ran aground and the crew abandoned ship. The other two, seeing this, fled. This led the pirates to conclude that Havana had no serious defense, and they went back. The people offered them another six hundred ducados, but this time the pirates were in no hurry to leave. They sacked the town for fifteen days, taking everything of value they could find, even the church bells.

The Spanish decided to fortify the city, building a castle by the opening of the harbor. The next pirate ship, a British one, landed further down the coast and avoided the harbor fortress by attacking from inland. The townspeople fled the city and hid out in the bush while their town was plundered.

Such raids became a way of life in Havana. As new streets were added, they continued to be made very narrow, because this was thought to be more defensible. Every Habanero man was required to carry a sword at all times.

In July 1555, a French pirate named Jacques de Sores arrived. His reputation was so great that England's Queen Elizabeth competed with France's François I for his services. Historians disagree on the number of ships under his command. Some say as few as two, others as many as twenty.

These pirates took Havana in about thirty minutes. The governor, Gonzalo Pérez de Angulo, gathered up his family and household goods and quickly resettled on the other side of the bay, in what is now the section of eastern Havana called Guanabacoa. But Juan de Lobera, the commander of the fort, stayed and asked for volunteers to defend it. He amassed a force of sixteen—some Spanish, some African, and even a few Tainos. Even then, Habaneros came in many colors.

They held out, locked in the fort, preventing ships from entering the harbor and even managing to shoot down a

French flag the pirates had planted. When de Sores set the fort on fire, they finally surrendered. They had fought so hard that de Sores was convinced they had been guarding a fortune hidden in the fort. But all he found was the governor's personal possessions, a small amount of cash, and his wife's emerald ring. They took it, of course.

They searched the city and found little. The fabled treasure was never in the town, but rather in a fleet that was not there at the time. The pirates then attempted to ransom the citizenry, but failed. Finally, they slit the throats of many of their hostages, burned the city to the ground, torched all the ships in the bay, and even destroyed large swaths of the countryside. Leaving Havana a blackened patch smoking by the sea, with its few survivors choking in the remains, they sailed away.

There was little left of the town, but the townspeople rebuilt. Before the construction was even completed, another French pirate came and burned it down again. The Spanish responded by calling for a huge stone fortress, the Castillo de la Real Fuerza, to be built on the western side of the harbor opening. King Philip II sent a leading military engineer, Bartolomé Sánchez, and forty stonemasons to work on the project. All the Spanish colonies contributed money, because they wanted a fort that would protect their goods. But there was not nearly enough labor to build the fortress.

By this time, the Spanish had been bringing enslaved Africans to Cuba for fifty years, mostly to work in agriculture. The crown commandeered the African slaves in the fields to work on building the fortress for a while, but this abruptly halted agricultural production and created food shortages. It even became difficult to provision ships. Then the crown ordered all the blacks who had managed to obtain freedom and had moved to Havana to escape agricultural labor to report for work or receive one hundred lashes. Freedom, it seemed, was a relative concept.

The fortress was finally completed in 1582.

In 1589, to add even more security, a tower and fortress were built at the eastern opening of the harbor. This was the high ground that had been used to warn of oncoming ships even before any fortifications were built. Named Castillo de los Tres Reyes Magos del Morro, after the three kings at the birth of Christ, it is now usually called simply El Morro, which means "the high ground." Another fortress, La Punta, was later built directly across from the Morro, on the very tip of the western side of the harbor, just up from the Castillo. The harbor entrance was now guarded by three fortresses.

Still, more pirate raids came. And so every night a huge iron chain with wooden beams would be suspended between the two forts, across the opening of the harbor, to prevent ships from entering.

And still the pirates came. Two more small fortresses were built on the coast. In 1674, a wall around the city was begun, but it would be another century before Havana was entirely walled off. The completed wall was five feet thick

ENTRANCE TO THE HARBOR OF HAVANA.

The opening of Havana harbor and the Morro seen from Habana Vieja in June 1877. Frank Leslie's Popular Monthly

and thirty-three feet high, with nine gates to be locked every night. But even with the fortresses, the wall, the gates, and the chained-off harbor, for those staring out to sea, it seemed certain that more trouble would come.

•

EARLY HAVANA WAS a poorly maintained city. The streets were filthy, and there was as much mud as there was cobblestone. The Plaza de la Catedral, one of five main squares in Habana Vieja, was built on a low-lying, poorly drained spot that flooded after every rainfall. Apparently Havana humor was already fully developed, because the popular name for the stately plaza was Plazuela de la Ciénaga — the little plaza in the swamp.

The Spanish had originally favored Santiago, in the eastern part of the island, the part closest to Spain, for their

Plaza de la Catedral. The Drawing-Room Companion, *1851*

capital and main port. But from Santiago, a ship had to sail up the coast to Guantánamo and then through the treacherous Windward Passage between Cuba and Haiti to get to the Atlantic. From Havana, by contrast, a ship had simply to leave the harbor.

Starting in the sixteenth century, Atlantic trade became the mainstay of international commerce. Cuba's export economy at the time was centered around cattle—beef and, especially, leather. Historical novelist Antonio Benítez Rojo aptly called leather "the plastic of its day." Leather was ubiquitous. Most everything had leather in it. The rich, subtropical pasturelands of eastern Cuba produced hides that were thicker, shinier, and far superior to the leather produced from European pastures. The leather was primarily shipped from Havana, but it was Santiago and its prosperous eastern provinces that developed most rapidly, while Havana and its environs remained a backwater.

But late in the sixteenth century, the island's political and economic center of gravity began to shift when sugar, previously viewed as an amusement for a handful of wealthy people in Europe, became a European obsession. Sugar, despite its expensive dependence on African slave labor, became more profitable than leather, and the crop was produced in the west, in the areas around Havana.

At the end of the sixteenth century, the Spanish monarchy promoted San Cristóbal de la Habana, the port village of vice, mud, and stench, from a town to an official city— more in recognition of its potential than of the reality. In 1607, the capital of the colony of Cuba was moved from Santiago to Havana.

Havana grew as a commercial port. By the eighteenth century it was shipping sugar, leather, and tobacco—adding a new redolence to its infamous smells—and there was tremendous international demand for Cuban tropical hardwood. More and more Africans were being brought in as slaves to produce these profitable goods cheaply, especially sugar.

When a shipyard was built in Havana in 1723, the port also became a major center of shipbuilding. Between 1724 and 1796, 114 Spanish military ships were constructed there. Havana-built ships were in great demand, because

Cuban wood was thought to be vastly superior to that of Europe.

By the end of the eighteenth century, life in Havana society was much less egalitarian than it had been a hundred years earlier. Cuban settlers who accumulated wealth built mansions, claiming they were descended from conquistadors and giving themselves titles, often fictitious ones that included the names of Cuban towns or provinces.

Havana now had several large churches built of stone, and its narrow streets were lined with substantial stone-walled homes with tile roofs. The architects, as in much of Latin America, had come from Andalusia, in southern Spain, which had been under the control of Muslims for eight hundred years before the Christians drove them out in 1492. The Arab-influenced architecture they brought was designed for a hot climate.

The houses the Andalusians designed had huge, ornate carved wooden doorways. The interiors were dark, with few windows to let in the hot sunlight. What little light entered was diffused by stained glass semicircles of deeply colored geometric panes above a doorway or window.

At the center of each house was an outdoor patio, tiled and well-gardened with flowers, vines, and potted palms. Parties and most social events were held in the patio, which was the coolest place in the house.

The new houses were usually two stories high. The ground floor was used for storage and sometimes had a shop or two. The ground floor also had slave quarters. The family lived

*The Palacio de los Capitanes Generales in the Plaza de Armas
looking much the way it does in its restored condition today.*
Illustrated London News, *August 21, 1869*

on the second floor, with balconies overlooking the street, as
well as a gallery—a covered balcony above the patio.

•

BY THE MID-EIGHTEENTH century, with the city fortified
with solid houses that would not easily burn, three
fortresses, and a wall, the Habaneros seemed to be safe.
The Spanish had a strong military presence. In the Plaza
de Armas, the governor-general ruled from the high-
ceilinged, red-draped "throne room" of the Palacio de los
Capitanes Generales. And Habaneros were prospering,
thanks to their busy port.

But then, on June 7, 1762, a British invasion force of more than eleven thousand troops landed in Cojímar, a small port a few miles east of Havana. Commodore Augustus Keppel rallied his troops, waving his hat, and promised fruitful looting, offering the inspiring sentiment that after they took "yonder town . . . we shall all be as rich as Jews!" After months of bitter fighting, reinforcements from North America arrived, including troops that in a few years would fight against the British for American independence. On August 13, the Spanish surrendered Havana.

To the Habaneros, this was a terrifying experience and a bitter defeat, a tragic disaster. They called the British troops "mameyes," after a red-fleshed tropical fruit. To this day, a moment of reckoning—the angry wife coming home, or the boss calling someone to account—is called *la hora de los mameyes* (the hour of the mameyes).

The memory lingered, though the British didn't. During the two-month siege, the Spanish had moved the booty off-shore, leaving little for the British soldiers to loot. London had no real interest in Havana anyway; it was just a pawn to be traded in negotiations. Less than a year later, in July 1763, the last of the mameyes were loaded onto ships and Havana was returned to Spain. In the Treaty of Paris signed by Britain, Spain, and France just a few months earlier, Havana had been traded back to the Spanish in exchange for Florida. William Pitt, the Elder, both a past and future British prime minister, argued that it was a bad trade. That controversy has never been resolved.

THREE

Danger of a Black City

＊

"¡Acabar con los negros!" repitió D. Candido fingiendo sor-
presa. "No hará tal, por la sencilla razón de que de ellos está
llena el Africa."

"Kill off all the blacks!" Don Candido repeated, feigning
surprise. "He won't do any such thing, for the simple reason that Africa is full of them."

— CIRILO VILLAVERDE, *Cecilia Valdés* (1882)

WHAT SHAPED AND defined Cuba, and shaped and
defined Havana, and yet has made them different,
is slavery. It has at times been suggested that the impact of
slavery on modern Cuba is exaggerated, but so profound
and fundamental is slavery to the identity of both Havana
and Cuba that it would be almost impossible to overstate it.

Slavery lasted longer in Cuba than anywhere else in
the Americas. When I first visited the country in the early
1980s, it was still possible to meet Cubans who had known
their African-born grandparents. Slavery was not abolished in Cuba until a Spanish royal decree on October 7,
1886. This means that when Fidel Castro came to power on
January 1, 1959, slavery had been abolished for only sev-
enty-two years. Cuba had been separated from its colonial

mother country for only sixty years. The slave owners had opposed Cuban independence, and it was their grandchildren who made up a large part of the wealthy oligarchy that initially opposed Fidel Castro's revolution.

The Spanish began the African slave trade to the Americas. Christopher Columbus's son Diego is thought to have started it in Santo Domingo in 1505, but some records indicate that Africans were being brought over as early as 1501. In 1513, Amador de Lares, a wealthy landowner in Cuba, was given permission to bring in four African slaves from nearby Hispaniola (the island now shared by the Dominican Republic and Haiti). This request is the oldest record of slavery in Cuba. Spanish Hispaniola and Spanish Cuba were the first African slave colonies in the Americas, but slavery in the former was abolished in 1822—much earlier than in Cuba.

In 1533, Cuba had its first slave uprising in a mine in Jobabo, in the eastern part of the island. The Spanish decapitated the rebels and put their heads on display.

The whites feared the Africans, and tried to control them with terror. Rebellion aside, the worst fates were met by those who ran away, and yet slaves did run away regularly. Havana newspapers listed them in a column marked "*esclavos profúgos*" (fugitive slaves). A captured runaway would be mutilated and beaten nearly to death. Runaways would kill themselves rather than be taken. Sometimes they succeeded in hanging themselves or poisoning themselves. Eating enough dirt would sometimes work. If they had no other means available, according to contemporary accounts, they would sometimes swallow their tongues and choke to death. A common belief among the slaves was that in death they would be carried back to Africa, back to freedom.

The more the slaves were abused, the more they rebelled and the more the whites feared them, and then they were abused even more. The whites believed that the slaves were primitive creatures who hated them and could be controlled only by fear. José Martí championed abolition and once wrote, "Only those who hate the Negro see hatred in the Negro."

•

DESPITE BEING ONE of the first slave colonies, Cuba had a relatively small slave population compared with other Caribbean colonies, such as Haiti and Jamaica, at the time the British took Havana in 1762. It was the British who made Havana a huge slave-trading center. To begin with, they brought in twelve hundred slaves to use in the siege of Havana, and after they took the city they established a slave market in which to sell them off. So although Cuban slave labor was used primarily in agricultural regions outside the city, the slave trade became centered in Havana.

By the early nineteenth century, when the city was firmly back in Spanish control, it was generating an enormous amount of wealth. This was no longer due to treasures being shipped from Latin America to Europe, but to the slave trade and the growing sugar trade. The bigger the sugar market, the more sugar was produced, and the more slaves were needed to work the plantations. The most accepted estimate is that 65 percent of the slaves in Cuba worked in sugar production and another 15 percent in other forms of agriculture.

The slaves literally had nothing. They were issued crude garments to wear. At harvest time, they worked sixteen hours every day. Many died from exhaustion, but the slave owners considered it cheaper to buy new slaves than to care for the ones already bought.

The slave owners lived in extravagant mansions that can still be seen in Habana Vieja—some so large that they have been turned into hotels. The wealthy fretted over their luxuries, clothing, and jewelry and what to wear to dances and the theater. They attended concerts and operas, including a few by Havana-born composers and musicians of distinction. White people in Havana had one of the highest standards of living in the Americas. Their lives were full not only of European luxuries but also of American technology. Because of the needs of the sugar industry, Cuba had a railroad system, built with the help of American engineers, even before Spain did.

Both slave and free black populations increased enormously in the nineteenth century. In 1790, Cuba had 153,559 whites, 64,590 slaves, and 54,151 "free people of color." By 1869 there were 763,176 whites, 363,286 slaves, and 238,927 "free coloreds."

The slaves were off-loaded by the shipload in the Havana port where the sugar and tobacco were being on-loaded. They were then placed in conveniently located barracoons—one in town, and one out in the woodlands, near parks and outdoor recreation areas. The train that ran into Havana passed by the woodlands barracoon, and travelers could entertain themselves by looking out the window at the caged Africans. Since the Africans had never seen a train before, they were often terrified and flailed their arms in ways that the travelers found amusing. Families took carriage rides to view the Africans in their cages.

Slavery revealed the barbarism behind the front of gentility. Sale days were not for family outings. The men who were prospective buyers were kept behind a locked door, listening to the wails and groans on the other side. Finally the door was opened and the men elbowed their way inside, struggling to grab as many "choice ones," mostly naked men, as they could manage to hold by hand or rope.

•

AN ODDITY IN Spanish law, and one that had a huge impact on Havana, granted slaves the ability to buy their freedom. All slaves had a fixed value and could either purchase themselves outright or pay in installments, becoming part owners of themselves. It was a right guaranteed by law.

Of course, "right" here is a murky term. To buy freedom, the slave had to have money, and earning money was not a guaranteed right of slaves. Slaves from the sugar fields had few opportunities to earn money, but in Havana there were many possibilities. Unlike the field slaves, the slaves who worked in households in Havana were predominantly women. Both male and female slaves in Havana could sell something on the street, including their bodies, which is how Havana became Cuba's center of prostitution. There were many other commercial possibilities as well, including running a small shop.

This resulted in three very important differences between Havana and the rest of Cuba. Havana had far more free blacks than any other part of the island. It also had more women. And it had far more people of mixed race, who were considered exotic—especially the women, *las mulatas*.

The city's economy depended on the labor of free blacks. Not only were cooks, tailors, launderers, and carpenters free blacks, but some of Havana's most celebrated industries, such as shipbuilding and cigar making, depended on free black labor. In the late eighteenth and nineteenth centuries, when cigar production became industrialized and quality "Havanas" became popular in Europe and North America, the rollers were mostly free blacks.

The rest of Cuba had a shortage of women. The white men coming from Spain to seek their fortune often came without women. But there was a greater imbalance in the slave population. Most slaves were men who had been brought over between the ages of fifteen and twenty. Slave owners wanted slaves primarily for hard manual labor and, with the exception of the few women used as house slaves, mostly in Havana homes, did not want women.

The ability of Havana house slaves to earn money on the side to buy their freedom was only one of the factors contributing to a large free black population in the city. Another was the tendency of slave owners to have sex with their female slaves. The sex was sometimes obtained by physical force, sometimes by intimidation, sometimes by promises of better living conditions, and sometimes by all three. If the union resulted in a child, the woman might be freed, though often she was sold as a wet nurse. But the child was automatically considered free.

This also occurred on plantations, though there were fewer slave women there. And since no one would stay on a sugar plantation if they didn't have to, freed blacks often drifted into cities. The great magnet was Havana, with its large free population, and so the city became known for its black population, its black culture. From music to religion to a distinct way of speaking, Havana has remained the center for African culture in Cuba.

•

AT THE END of the eighteenth century, the worst nightmare of slave owners everywhere occurred. The Haitian slaves rose up and overwhelmed their masters in a prolonged bloodbath that ended slavery there and drove white people out of Haiti. Many of the French planters who managed to escape relocated to Cuba, bringing with them horrifying stories.

Cuba had its own history of slave rebellions. The 1533 Jobabo mine uprising had been only the beginning. In 1727, the slaves at the Quiebra Hacha plantation, just south of Havana, rose up, left the plantation with tools and firearms, and terrorized the surrounding area, plundering and killing. The rebellion was put down by a well-armed contingent of infantry from Havana.

The reason Cuba remained a Spanish colony for more than a half-century longer than the rest of Latin America was that its slave owners wanted, and obtained, a Spanish military presence on the island. The slave owners were afraid of not only their slaves but also of Cuba's many free blacks, who were more difficult to suppress than slaves were.

Alexander von Humboldt, a noted Prussian geographer, made a number of trips to Cuba in the early nineteenth century. He observed with alarm that by 1825 the slave and free black populations were on their way to outnumbering the white population. "The free blacks, who may easily make common cause with the slaves, increase rapidly in Cuba," he warned.

Von Humboldt cautioned that the situation in Havana was particularly troubling, partly because free blacks from other parts of Cuba were drifting into the capital. He stated that in twenty years the white population of Havana had increased by 73 percent, whereas the "free colored" population had increased by 171 percent.

The Cuban slave owners' nightmare of a white bloodbath nearly happened. In 1812, a free black from Havana, José Antonio Aponte, led a black uprising. He was a priest of the Yoruba spirit, Changó, who used African religion to spread his movement—something that whites had always suspected and feared would happen.

Aponte's uprising, occurring just eight years after the Haitian Revolution, invoked the names of that revolt's leader, Toussaint Louverture, and the other heroes of Haiti. One of the organizers in eastern Cuba, Hilario Herrera, was actually a veteran of the Haitian Revolution.

The uprising was island-wide; its goal was the abolition of slavery and ultimately the overthrow of Spanish rule. Revolts took place in Havana and most major cities, as well as on rural plantations. But Aponte was betrayed by disloyal followers and captured and hanged, along with eight others. After death, they were decapitated, and their heads were placed in cages around the city. One of Aponte's hands was also displayed. *"Mas malo que Aponte"* (worse than Aponte) became a popular expression in Havana for doing something that was really bad.

The fear continued, as did the slavery. In 1844, the Spanish government claimed to have broken a conspiracy known as La Conspiración de la Escalera (the Ladder Conspiracy), because many of the accused were tied to ladders and beaten. Thousands of slaves, free blacks, and mulatos were sent into exile, beaten, imprisoned, or executed, and it is still not clear whether an uprising actually had been planned or whether this was just an attempt by the government to crush the abolition movement.

In 1817, the Spanish signed an agreement with the British to curtail the dangerous practice of importing Africans, but then the sugar market expanded, so slaves were smuggled in. Another treaty banning the importation of slaves was signed with the British in 1835, but the smuggling continued. By the mid-1800s, fifty thousand African slaves were being smuggled into Cuba every year. When the smugglers were caught at sea, they would simply toss their human cache overboard. With profits as high as 200 percent on a slave bought in Africa and sold in Havana, traders could afford to throw a few hundred away.

FOUR

Cecilia's Fire and Sugar

La complexión podía pasar por saludable, la encarnación viva,
hablando en el sentido en que los pintores toman esta palabra,
aunque a poco que se fijaba la atención, se advertía en el color
del rostro, que sin dejar de ser sanguíneo, había demasiado ocre
en su composición, y no resultaba diáfano ni libre. ¿A qué raza,
pues, pertenecía esta muchacha?

Her complexion could pass for healthy, with a ruddiness,
speaking in the sense of this word used by painters,
although once it was looked at closely, it could be seen that
healthy glow aside, there was too much ocher in the color
of her face, as a result of which her complexion was neither
translucent nor free of other shadings. Then to what race
did this girl belong?

— CIRILO VILLAVERDE, *Cecilia Valdés* (1882)

THE FREE BLACK population in Havana was about half
women, sometimes even more than half women,
because a woman slave was worth only a third of the
value of a man, which made it much easier for women
to buy their freedom. By contrast, women remained
scarce in the countryside; slavers didn't want pregnant women or babies, because they were not very
productive.

Havana became known as a city full of women—beautiful women. By extension, it is sometimes credited with beautiful men, but the emphasis has usually been on its women. In *Our Man in Havana*, Graham Greene comments, "To live in Havana was to live in a factory that turned out human beauty on a conveyor-belt."

What most attracts many Habaneros, at least according to them—they talk about this constantly—is that some of these women are, as they say, "*muy atrás*," endowed with ample posteriors. References to this are ubiquitous not only in conversation and song lyrics but also in literature. In Edmundo Desnoes's 1965 novel *Inconsolable Memories*, the narrator says, in seeming seriousness, "The S formed by the stomach and the ass reaches a point in certain Cuban women where it becomes independent, out of proportion with the rest of the body, even having its own personality."

Piropos, the catcalls men shout out at attractive women on Havana streets, are often odes to the ampleness of posteriors, how they are palaces, how they are revolutionary, how there is no shortage there—depending on what the political mood of the moment is. The woman's response—amusement, embarrassment, anger—depends on her mood of the moment but when it is well-aimed social commentary, that is usually appreciated.

Inevitably, the city with this kind of reputation for beautiful women became known for its sex industry. During colonial times, and again during post-independence dictatorships—especially under the 1952–1959 reign of Fulgencio Batista, who had strong American Mafia ties—prostitution grew into a hugely profitable enterprise, with rows of houses of ill repute, girlie shows at the downtown Shanghai Theater, and lots of cheesecake in the clubs. Until it was torn down shortly after the revolution, the Plaza del Vapor was a huge prostitute market.

After Fidel Castro came to power in 1959, being slightly feminist, extremely prudish, and, besides, opposed to free enterprise, he tried to shut it all down. But in the more than half a century since he took power, the Cuban government has not succeeded in ending prostitution. It turns up wherever foreigners do, around certain hotels and certain restaurants, because many foreign men still dream of a night or even a few hours with an Habanera. Street pimps approach the foreigner and whisper, *"Quieres una mu-la-ta?"* In Havana street language, infamous for skipping syllables and dropping phonemes, the word *mulata* is three carefully enunciated syllables.

Since at least the late eighteenth century, when slavery became large-scale, there has been a mystique about the mulata. Could there be a more typically Habanero myth than the legend that Havana cigars are rolled on the thighs of mulatas? In reality, they aren't rolled on thighs; women were not even employed in cigar factories until 1877. The myth was started by a French journalist.

The mystique of the mulata, rooted in the racism and sexism of the slave society, started with the fact that a mulata was someone who had never been a slave and, being half white, would have been considered a nearly full-fledged human being. The difference in the standings of a black woman and a mulata was reflected in nineteenth-century men's slang. A mulata was called "a cinnamon," something exotic and delicious; a black woman was called "a coal."

It may be that many people find people of mixed race to be attractive. The Spanish poet García Lorca said that Havana had the most beautiful women in the world and wrote that the reason was "owing to the drops of black blood that all Cubans carry."

But the Havana mulata also derived her reputation from her circumstance. Mulatas and mulatos, wanting to rise on the social ladder, had to be resourceful. In the 1950s, Cuban ethnographer Lydia Cabrera made a study of Cuban expressions that were modeled after African refrains. One was "Necessity is the father of the mulato."

A mulata was a woman with a higher social standing than a free black's, but lower than a white's. A person of mixed race was still a person of color, although one with more rights than a black. People of color were not accepted in certain jobs. They could not have the better seats at theaters and could not be seated at all in some restaurants. They were subject to petty humiliations, such as the omission of the title "Don" or "Doña" from their names on documents. Like most people in the middle of a social scale, people of mixed race attached great importance to

A crowd seems to swirl around an intriguing mulata *in this illustration of a masked ball*. The Graphic, *June 24, 1876*

moving up, and for mulatas, the key to this was white men. If a mulata had a child by a white man, that child would be a quadroon, which is the next-higher social position on the racist ladder.

Wealthy white Habaneros who did not have qualms about marital infidelity knew that beautiful mulatas were available. It was something that everyone in Havana knew but about which they preferred not to speak. A wealthy scion of a sugar family might sleep with his mulata, bestow to her seemingly endless gifts, and even provide her with a good Havana home, but if she demanded too much, he could get rid of her. So the mulata had to learn how to play her part carefully. She survived by being appealing.

A popular nineteenth-century song, or *guaracha*, about a mulata begins, *"Yo soy la reina de las mujeres"*:

> *I am the queen of women*
> *In this promised land.*
> *I am made of sugar and fire;*
> *I am the key to the heart.*

And then the refrain:

> *I don't know what I have here*
> *Nor what afflicts me.*
> *Ay, ay, ay!*
> *There is no cure for my sickness.*

> *I am the reason why men*
> *Don't love their little white women.*
> *Because they die for certain parts of me,*
> *And I melt them with my warmth.*

•

THE BEST WAY to understand the culture of the mulata in nineteenth-century Havana is to read the great gift left to us by Cirilo Villaverde—his novel *Cecilia Valdés*.

More than a generation older than Martí, Villaverde was born in 1812, the year of the Aponte slave uprising, in the western province of Pinar del Río. He was the son of a country doctor who lived on a sugar plantation, and in his early childhood he witnessed and was horrified by the brutality of plantation slavery. When he grew up, he moved to Havana, where he was educated and received a law degree while also starting a career as a writer. In 1848, when he became involved in a failed attempt to overthrow Spanish rule, he was arrested and sentenced to hard labor on a chain gang, but he managed to escape and settled in New York. There he lived and wrote for the rest of his life, more than forty years. He lived to see the end of slavery in Cuba but died in 1894, four years before the overthrow of the Spanish.

Villaverde first wrote *Cecilia Valdés* in Havana in 1839, and then rewrote it. He rewrote it several more times in New York. The story became longer and more complicated each time. He did not finally publish it until 1882, and then only in New York. It could not be published in Cuba until after independence, in 1903, and has had more than fifteen editions since then. In the frustrating world of post-revolution Cuban state publishing, where a wide variety of books come out but few stay in print more than a moment if they're not about Fidel or Che (or both together), *Cecilia Valdés* is always available.

It has been said that *Cecilia Valdés* is the Cuban *Uncle Tom's Cabin*, and it is true that it is a searing condemnation of slavery and slavery's impact on society. But while

Harriet Beecher Stowe's book spearheaded the abolitionist movement and has since become a seldom-read historical artifact, *Cecilia Valdés* came out at the end of the abolition struggle and has become a centerpiece of the canon of Cuban literature.

Villaverde, like many Cuban exiles after him, spent his life longing for a world he would not see again, and as he revised his book, he moved beyond the issue of slavery to the social ills created by slavery that seemed certain to outlast it—issues such as racism and the unfair treatment of women, issues that, in fact, have remained. He dedicated his novel "To the Women of Cuba."

There are certain novels—*Don Quixote* in Spain, *Les Misérables* in France, *War and Peace* in Russia, and *Huckleberry Finn* in the United States—that become central to the cultural identity of a nation. In Cuban literature, it is *Cecilia Valdés*. José Martí, who is generally considered to be Cuba's greatest writer, thought Villaverde's book was an unforgettable masterpiece. As with *Huckleberry Finn* and all books that achieve national importance, there are constant criticisms of *Cecilia Valdés*, but if you want to talk about Cuban literature, this book, along with a few poems, essays, and letters of Martí, has to be read.

•

CECILIA HAS BECOME the enduring image of the Havana mulata. Her beauty is breathtaking. Sugar and fire, she melts black, brown, and white men with her warmth. She is not particularly a schemer, but, being an orphan, she does have to look out for herself, which means having a wealthy white suitor. The scion of a sugar-wealthy aristocratic family has fallen in love with her. And she loves him. He, of course, is not supposed to marry a mulata; he is engaged to the white daughter of another aristocratic family.

Cecilia thinks she is an orphan—Valdés was a last name often given to orphans in that era—but actually her mother is a slave and her father is the father of her wealthy lover. So they are half siblings without knowing it. The father has to stop this union without revealing that he has a mulata daughter. Cecilia does not understand that the game is rigged against her.

The mother of the fine young man who loves Cecilia is a lady of apparently refined sensibilities who does not enjoy family vacations at the *ingenio*, as a sugar mill in Cuba is called, where slaves are worked to death. She does not oppose slavery, and accepts the argument that slaves have to be punished, beaten nearly to death or mutilated because they are too barbarous to comprehend anything else, but she doesn't like to see it. She is soft. "Enough of your belief that bundles from Africa have a soul and are angels," her husband says to her.

•

As IN THE rest of the Caribbean, the straightness of hair, the thickness of lips, the shading of fingernails—every possible physical characteristic—were examined as clues to everyone's exact racial mixture. The coloring of hands or the shape of the nose was often considered to be a certain tip-off.

In the case of Cecilia, the beautiful orphan of unknown parentage, we are told, "A knowing eye could not help noticing that her red lips had a dark border or edging, and that the bright glow of her face ended in a sort of half shadow near her hairline."

One of the more interesting examples of these kinds of observations—still made of friends, neighbors, employers, and political figures by Habaneros today—is that the face of the dictator Batista indicated to connoisseurs of racism the presence of Taino blood; Taino blood was once considered almost as damning as African blood. Before coming to power, Batista had been excluded from certain clubs for being Taino, even though there were supposedly no more Tainos. "You could see it in his face," it was said.

•

Now that decades have passed since the abolition of slavery in Cuba, the conversation in Havana has shifted, but only slightly. People still joke about one another's suspect features. *"El que no tiene de Congo tiene de Carabalí"* is a common Havana expression—"Those who don't have some Congo in them have some Carabalí." Both are Cuban terms for African ethnicities.

In the mid-twentieth century, anthropologist Fernando Ortiz observed that Havana men judged Havana women the same way that they judged Havana cigars. Tobacco, he observed, "the product of infinite crossbreeding and mixtures," came in many different colors. No two cigars were alike, and all smokers had their preferred colors— "claros, colorado-claros, colorados, colorado-maduros," and so on—a very long list. "The color of the different types of cigar," Ortiz noted, "like that of women, cannot be simply reduced to blondes and brunettes." Ortiz analyzed both the racism and sexism (which Cubans prefer to call *machismo*) in Cuba, but also noted that bantering about race and sex was broadly accepted as a way of speaking and of joking without malice.

Habaneros still enjoy the word game of labeling racial distinctions. They frequently call a friend "negrito," which, though it can be used as an offensive term, can also be said with humor and without rancor—a term of endearment—at least when said by one person of color about another person of color. In the Spanish language, adding a diminutive to a pejorative detoxifies the word and gives it a humorous and ironic twist. Another term of friendship, now a bit old-fashioned, is *chino*, which literally means a Chinese man, but in Havana street slang means a person of mixed blood and is used to indicate a friend, like "buddy." There is also plenty of bantering about *blanquitos*. Often an Habanero will make up their own term. Poet Virgilio Piñera used to quip that he was an "*altísimo mulato blanco-nozo*," which roughly translates to "a light mulato who is white but not really."

Should a *negrita* and a *blanquito*, or a *negrito* and a *blan-quita*, decide to get married, the union, which is commonly called "rice and beans," is generally accepted without controversy. There are more people of mixed blood, and fewer and fewer whites and blacks, with each passing year. Current estimates are that only about 40 percent of the people in Havana are of pure European stock. Some studies show a higher percentage of whites, and some a lower percentage, but few show a white majority.

Racism has certainly not vanished and the weight of history in many ways gives economic advantage to those with lighter skin. For example, since the majority of exiles who send goods and money to relatives in Cuba happen to be white, their white relatives are the recipients of this largess and few black people are getting gifts from Miami. Still, Havana is an increasingly mixed society and racial differences are most often material for humor.

FIVE

Beyond the Wall

Havana is a really big city. That's what my mother says
and she knows a lot about these things. They say that a
child can get lost in it forever. That two people can be
looking for each other for years and never meet. But I
like my city.

— MIRTA YÁÑEZ, *La Habana Es una Ciudad Bien
Grande* (1980)

HAVANA WAS, AND Habana Vieja still is, a city of narrow streets—laid out for either easier defense or more
shade—and of sidewalks so narrow that a pedestrian can
barely walk on them. Richard Henry Dana Jr., famous for
his exposé on the merchant marine, *Two Years Before the
Mast*, noted in 1859:

> The streets are so narrow and the houses built so close
> upon them that they seem to be rather spaces between
> the walls of houses than highways for travel. It seems
> impossible that two vehicles should pass abreast, yet
> they do so. There are constant blockings of the way.
> In some places awnings are stretched over the entire
> street, from house to house, and we are riding under
> a long tent.

Narrow sidewalk in Habana Vieja. Frank Leslie's Popular
Monthly, *August 1878*

Women with their full skirts could never walk on the
sidewalks, and the streets were muddy and filled with dangerous traffic. "Real ladies," that is to say white women,
didn't walk outside in any event. Only women of color
were seen on the street, and it is easy to imagine the allure
of women of color who could go anywhere, drink, gam-
ble, and even, according to many accounts, smoke cigars.
Twentieth-century Cuban writer Guillermo Cabrera
Infante claimed that cigar bands, which were invented in

1830 by Gustav Bock, a German immigrant, for his Aguila de Oro cigars, were created so that women would not have to touch the tobacco leaf while smoking.

White women stayed home and sat in windows like pretty birds in cages. Windows were tall, situated just slightly above the street, and covered with iron gratings. They didn't, and still don't, have any glass, allowing breezes to pass through.

These windows were always a subject of fascination for visitors, not only for the way in which beautiful and finely dressed women carried on courtships with suitors outside in plain view, but also for the way in which, on hot nights, whole families would be on display in their open windows. Anthony Trollope wrote that families "pass their evening seated near the large low open window of their drawing-rooms; and as these windows almost always look into the street, the whole internal arrangement is seen by every one who passes." Dana wrote, "The windows come to the ground, and, being flush with the street, and mostly without glass, nothing but the grating prevents a passenger from walking into the rooms."

Meanwhile, people of color were working, out on the street, trying to be resourceful. Travelers such as Trollope, Dana, and nineteenth-century travel writer Samuel Hazard confirm this.

Wealthy young white men busied themselves with empty amusements. "The young men," wrote Trollope,

Courtship at a Havana window. Harper's Weekly, *May 3, 1873*

"and many of those who are no longer young, spend their evenings, and apparently a large portion of their days, in eating ices and playing billiards."

When wealthy young white women wanted to go out, they would go for a ride in a volante. Volantes were conveyances, designed specifically for young women, about which virtually all nineteenth-century visitors to Havana had to comment. A young woman would *never* descend from a volante until she returned home again, and then she would do so only when the volante pulled into her home's courtyard—never on the street. If she wanted to go shopping, her volante would stop in front of a store and the shop owner would come out to her.

The volante featured a kind of bucket-seat carriage that rode high on an axle between two enormous spoked wheels. Two extremely long shafts connected the wheels to a driver's seat far in front and to one or two horses.

The more aristocratic the lady, the greater the distance between her seat and that of the driver, making for unwieldy vehicles navigating narrow streets. U-turns

Volantes in Habana Vieja. The Drawing-Room Companion, *1851*

were out of the question. Volantes could barely turn the tight corners of Habana Vieja, and, according to Samuel Hazard, an attempted turn was "the occasion of much hard swearing." Gentility has always been paper-thin in Havana.

It took some skill for two volantes arriving from opposite directions to pass: no wonder the sidewalks were so narrow. The slave who drove a volante, the *calesero*, was part of the decoration. He would be dressed in a velvet coat of scarlet or another deep color, festooned with gold or silver lace, spotless white breeches and waistcoat, a black silk hat with a silver or gold band, and brilliantly polished knee-high boots as shiny as glass. The horses' silver stirrups bore the master's coat of arms. The total effect was that of a fruit bowl of lovely women rolled through the streets in a decorative chariot.

In nineteenth-century Havana, carriages were important status symbols, much like Cadillacs in Havana in the 1950s—an opportunity for the wealthy to show off their standing. In the opening paragraph of *Cecilia Valdés*, a character asserts his position through the outfit of his driver and the silver ornament of his harnesses.

The passenger compartment was suspended with leather straps that absorbed shocks as the *calesero* pranced the horses down the bumpy streets at a good pace, forcing pedestrians to scramble out of the way. Many of the people on foot were people of color anyway, so the lack of adequate sidewalk space was considered of little importance.

·

BY THE NINETEENTH century, the old city wall could no longer hold Havana. This was due not only to a growing population but also to the bustle and drive of that population, who were not to be confined to one small corner sealed off by a wall. The streets were packed with three things Habaneros have always loved: bars, cafés, and casinos. And at night there were dances, because if there was anything that Habaneros loved more than drinking and gambling, it was dancing.

Who could resist such a place? Even in the nineteenth century, Havana was full of tourists. In fact, the city invented Caribbean tourism long before anywhere else, even carving out spacious rooms in the rocks by the sea—their remnants still visible today when the tide and waves are right—where visitors could bathe in ocean water in private spaces with ledges and rock seats to relax on while partially submerged. The rooms' openings allowed seawater to rush in but, according to Hazard, were small enough to keep out "any voracious monster." This may have been a reference to sharks, which abound in these waters. Habaneros did not make use of the rooms; they tended to think of them as some crazy thing that foreigners liked.

The city provided high-quality shopping in luxury stores on Calles Obispo and O'Reilly, named for an Irish-born Spanish military officer. China, glass, goods from Europe, silk, and cloth made from pineapple fiber were available under the shade-giving awnings. Today, as tourist shops are just beginning to reemerge, these same streets are a popular location.

At night, in addition to dances, Habaneros went to the opera. When the audience particularly appreciated a visiting singer, they would toss flowers. And then, if the performance had been especially fine, they would throw jewelry—good jewelry—pelting the singer with diamonds in that typical Havana way of overdoing things. The opera was not a place for moderation, but few places in Havana were.

Cockfights, featuring roosters hacking each other to death with the spurs on their feet while betting men screamed and shouted, were a favorite amusement in Havana. At a cockfight, the patina of gentility seen in the shops and theaters and opera houses was quickly peeled away. Hazard warned tourists, "Just pay one visit to a cock-fight, and I guarantee you'll not go again, but will come away intensely disgusted." But it was a place to see a cross section of Habanero society—slaves, free blacks, mulatos, poor whites, aristocrats.

The only people you didn't see were women.

•

IN 1827, A monument in honor of the founding of the city of Havana was completed in the Plaza de Armas, a prominent central location, in the style of an understated Greek temple with Doric columns. This set off a passion for neoclassical architecture. The wealthy yearned to build new houses with Doric or Ionic or even ornate Corinthian columns. But there was no available space within the walls of Havana. On the east side, the city butted up against the bay, with nowhere to grow. Only to the west, beyond the walls in undeveloped rural areas, was there space to build.

There, the Habaneros went column-mad. Alejo Carpentier wrote in 1982, "One of the most singular constants of Havana style: an incredible profusion of columns, a city that is a warehouse of columns, a jungle of columns, columns to infinity . . ." In strong sunlight, these columns suggested a film noir setting of darkly shaded *portales* (porticos), in which someone unseen could lurk and suddenly edge into the light.

As the city spread outside of its old walls and the decades passed by, every style of architecture from successive eras became popular—a process that continued into the twentieth century. Carpentier wrote, "The imposing of styles, the innovation of styles, good and bad, more bad than good, was creating in Havana this style without style." Today Havana is like a museum of architecture, exhibiting almost every idea from the early 1600s to the 1960s, with some good examples of each.

The westward expansion of Havana had actually already begun decades before the Habaneros went column-mad, in 1772, when the city built a grand boulevard

*A drawing of the Paseo del Prado with the Morro seen at the end.
By Childe Hassam for* Harper's Weekly *in 1895*

to the west of its walls. Unlike the streets in the rest of
Havana, it was broad, spacious, and well paved. It was
called the Paseo del Prado, after Madrid's great tree-lined
boulevard. From the far, inland end of the Havana boulevard, through the trees, could be seen the fort, the sea, and
the tower of the Morro. In 1877 a park, Parque Central,
was built alongside the thoroughfare.

Havana in the second half of the eighteenth century
contained more than forty thousand people—more
than New York City at that time. The wall had become
increasingly irrelevant. By the late eighteenth century,
Havana had two parts: *intramuros*, behind the wall,
which became Habana Vieja, and *extramuros*, outside the
wall, which is now known as Centro Habana. In 1863,

the demolition of the wall began, but that took almost as long as its construction had. The last of the wall was not torn down until the twentieth century. A fragment is preserved as a monument near the Habana Vieja house where José Martí spent his first four years of life; that house is also a museum.

SIX

The Monster

Viví en el monstruo, y le conozco las entrañas.

I lived in the monster, and I know its entrails.

— JOSÉ MARTÍ, on the United States in 1895

CUBA IN THE nineteenth century was marked by continual uprisings against Spanish rule. In 1823, an ex-soldier, José Francisco Lemus, organized an island-wide rebellion with the help of Masonic lodges. The plan was to establish an independent nation with the Taino name Cubanacán. But like the Aponte slave conspiracy of 1812, this rebellion was infiltrated by spies and failed.

After the uprising, Spain sent forty thousand troops to be permanently posted in Cuba. And those troops were on alert or at war for most of the rest of the century. *Peninsulares*, or people from Spain, as opposed to Cuban-born Spaniards, became increasingly disliked, except by the wealthy landowners, who believed that the troops would protect them from slaves, free blacks, and abolitionists, all of whom favored independence.

In 1851, Narciso López invaded Cuba. Born in Venezuela, he had fought against Simón Bolívar, the Venezuelan who tried to free South America from Spain and create a single united Latin American state. Though López had served as a local official for Spain in Cuba, he became enamored of the idea of having Cuba annexed by the United States. The Americans had long flirted with this idea. In 1808, Jefferson had sent an envoy to Havana to look into the possibility of buying the island, as he had done with the Louisiana Purchase. Nothing came of it, but by the 1840s, with rising tensions in the United States between slave and free states, there was some interest in the South in acquiring what would be an additional slave state. This of course meant that there was resistance to the idea among free blacks and abolitionists.

The greatest support for Narciso López in the United States came from proponents of Manifest Destiny, the much-contested belief that the white race should fulfill its destiny by taking over the North American continent. Some, such as John Quincy Adams, saw the belief as a conspiracy to spread slavery. Abraham Lincoln was one of its opponents. Manifest Destiny was the argument behind the 1846 U.S. invasion of Mexico and the seizure of almost half its territory.

López recruited American soldiers from the Mexican war and tried to get General Robert E. Lee or Colonel Jefferson Davis, both West Point Army officers, to lead them, but both declined. In 1850, López took command himself, invaded, and took the port of Cárdenas, east of Havana. But when the Spanish moved in troops, López and his army retreated by boat back to the United States.

The following year, López invaded again, with 435 volunteers, this time to the west of Havana. The Spanish captured or killed them all. In what seems a forerunner of the 1961 CIA-sponsored Bay of Pigs invasion, many were shot by firing squad; others were imprisoned and ransomed back to the United States. López was publicly garroted at La Punta fort, near Habana Vieja. Not far from where he was executed, what is possibly the shortest street in Habana Vieja was named Calle López in his honor. It runs into Calle Enna, named after the Spanish general who defeated him. López's flag had red and white stripes and a single star, based on the American flag. Strangely, that flag of annexation became the flag of Cuban independence and has remained, even today, the flag of Cuba.

•

NEW YORK, THE home of the exiled Havana intelligentsia, was the headquarters of the Cuban independence struggle, which began in 1868 with the bitter Ten Years' War. That war was unsuccessful, but after it ended, the intelligentsia started planning their next war, thus beginning a process that never stopped.

In New York, José Martí became both Cuba's "Apostle of Independence" and its most respected writer; he is still regarded as an important figure in Spanish-language literature. The most famous Habanero in history, he wrote most of his work in New York.

Guillermo Cabrera Infante, while himself living in exile from the Castro regime in London, wrote, perhaps not without envy, that no Cuban ever flourished more in exile than Martí, as he rose "from an obscure apprentice pamphleteer"—his status when he was deported at the age of nineteen—"into one of the greatest writers in the Spanish language and without any doubt into our prime prosist." Martí was prolific in exile. Today the Cuban government publishes his complete works in twenty-six volumes.

Cabrera Infante talks about the "denseness" of Martí's prose, comparing it to "solid metals like platinum." Martí wrote about politics and literature, about what he longed for and missed in Cuba, and about Cuban independence and the abolition of slavery. He also wrote about Emerson and Whitman, Ulysses Grant, Jesse James, Coney Island, and New York in the snow. The rare charm of his writing can be seen in the simple opening sentence of his essay on Charles Darwin: "Darwin was a grave old man who glowed with the pride of having seen."

Martí's poetry is thick with imagery and suggests a melancholy. As one of the first modernist poets of the Spanish language, he had a great influence on Spanish poetry. To read any of his writing—poetry or prose—is to revel in the sensuousness of someone who truly loved words. Those words are constantly quoted in the Spanish-speaking world, none more than the opening line of his collection *Simple Verses*:

> Yo soy un hombre sincero,
> de donde crece la palma.

I am an honest man,
from where the palm tree grows.

These are also the first words of one of the most popular Cuban songs ever written, "Guántanamera." The
song's popularity is surprising, given that no one is exactly
sure what it is about, though it clearly has nothing to do
with José Martí. It seems to be about unrequited love for
a woman from Guantánamo. It was written by a popular songwriter, Joseíto Fernández Diaz, probably around
1929. In the 1940s, he had a radio program called *La
Guántanama*, in which he used the song to introduce each
segment. He gave various explanations for who the peasant
woman from Guantánamo was. "Guajira Guántanamera,"
the chorus refrain, means a folk song from Guantánamo,
but Fernández never explained what José Martí or his
poem had to do with this. Many believe that Fernández
could not explain the lyrics well because he didn't actually write them, that they were written instead by noted
Spanish-born Cuban classical composer Julían Orbón. It
was Orbón who gave the song to Pete Seeger in a version
that included even more Martí verses, and that is the version Seeger popularized in America in the 1960s.

In time, the song faded away, as songs do, except among
Miami's Cuban exiles, the ones Castro called *gusanos*
(worms), whose *cubanidad* has been frozen in the Havana
of the 1950s. "They're still singing Guántanamera" was
a common Havana criticism of exiles. Today, however,

as tourists return to Havana in large numbers, the musicians in bars, restaurants, and hotels are playing "Guántanamera" again.

•

In 1892, Martí, still in New York, joined the Cuban Revolutionary Party, which began plotting another attempt to overthrow Spain. He argued for a Cuban government that represented all classes and races, and urged that it be established quickly, before the United States had time to intervene. If the Americans were to become involved, Martí predicted, they would seize control and never relinquish it.

Martí, who probably invented the term *latino*, or was certainly one of the first to use it, wrote an essay in 1891 called "Our America," by which he meant Latin America as opposed to that other America to the north. In that essay, he said that Latin America had to unite into one front and resist the United States. "Our America will be confronted by an enterprising and energetic nation seeking close relations, but with indifference and scorn for us and our ways," he wrote. He went on to say, "The scorn of our formidable neighbor, who does not know us, is the greatest danger for our America."

Martí helped raise money for an army to take Cuba, and in 1895 he returned to the island to join up with General Máximo Gómez. And so it was that this frail and balding forty-two-year-old Habanero turned New York poet, who neither rode horses well nor knew how to handle firearms, went off to war. He was thrilled to be out in the country- side, the way city people often are, fascinated by every leaf and bird chirp, and kept a diary that many consider his greatest writing.

General Gómez, a Dominican, was a battle-scarred pro- fessional soldier, trained in the Spanish army and a veteran of the Cuban independence fight. He had a bullet hole in his neck from the Ten Years' War that he still plugged up with cotton. During that struggle, he had earned a reputa- tion as a warrior of extraordinary physical courage and tac- tical savvy. His troops had been mostly black and mulato volunteers, and the Spanish had called them *"mambises,"* belittling them for their African heritage with a pejorative they had previously used for slaves in Santo Domingo. But their mockery backfired, and the name became popular among the independence troops.

Gómez combined a shortage of ammunition—only an estimated quarter of his troops had firearms—with what he knew to be a latent fear of black people among Spanish soldiers, to invent a tactic he called "the machete attack." Confronted with a line of Spanish infantry, his troops would fire once and then charge them on foot, Gómez in the lead, wielding machetes. Such charges terrified the Spanish soldiers.

Soon after Martí joined Gómez in eastern Cuba, there occurred a minor engagement with the enemy. Gómez ordered Martí to the rear. Instead the poet charged forward on horseback, carrying a handgun. Or was it that he had lost control of his horse?

In any event, he was shot in the neck, as Gómez had been in the Ten Years' War, done in by a sniper in the tall grass with a Remington rifle. In some versions, Martí died instantly; in another, a Spanish soldier on foot recognized him and finished him with a second bullet. And so the independence movement went to war without its spiritual leader, its "Apostle." In fact, his role as apostle was greatly aided by his martyrdom.

In the eastern hills of Cuba the day before Martí died, he started but never finished what would be his last letter. He was writing it to his friend Manuel Mercado, an under-secretary of the interior in the Mexican government. In his youth, in exile in Mexico with his parents, Martí had lived next door to Mercado, and the two had remained friends. In his letter, Martí wrote about his fears of a U.S. take-over of Cuba once the Spanish were gone. He knew that was likely, he said, because he had lived in the belly of the monster.

And indeed, the monster was itching to take Cuba. With its new imperialist might and the last of the Spanish empire crumbling, the United States dreamed of annexing Hawaii, the Philippines, Puerto Rico, and—the best prize of all, in their view—Cuba, the paradise right off their coast. This new round of Manifest Destiny enthralled an overwhelming majority of Americans, and President William McKinley, a true politician more than a true imperialist, could not resist the popular will. And so in 1898, the United States went to war with Spain in the Caribbean. They did exactly what Martí had feared: they drove out the Spaniards and took over. The poorly armed Cubans had fought Spain for nearly a century; they succumbed to the well-armed Americans in a four-month engagement.

On January 1, 1899, Spain withdrew from Cuba. That same day, a U.S. military government under General John R. Brooke took control.

The year before the takeover, an excited writer named Trumbull White had published a book called *Our New Possessions*, with sections on Cuba, Puerto Rico, Hawaii, and the Philippines. The section on Cuba, titled "The Pearl of the Antilles," began:

> The greatest island and the greatest city of all of the West Indies, discovered by Columbus on his first voyage, are now for the first time looking toward intimate commercial and social relations with the United States of America.

But "the greatest island" turned out to be somewhat of a disappointment. The Americans had not realized how run-down it was after generations of war. Health services, roads and bridges, schools and hospitals were in urgent need of improvements. The population, 1.5 million, had actually declined by two hundred thousand since the Cuban Revolutionary Party's war for independence began in 1895. According to an 1887 survey, only one in three white Cubans could write, and among people of color, only 11 percent were literate.

In December 1899, another general, Leonard Wood, took charge. This began phase two of the U.S. occupation. Wood had many plans. As a former U.S. surgeon general, he was interested in the research of a Cuban doctor, Carlos Juan Finlay, who had discovered that yellow fever is transmitted to humans by mosquitoes. Wood brought in U.S. Army doctor Walter Reed, whose work on parasites and tropical diseases, especially yellow fever, changed the history of medicine. The Americans also improved roads and bridges and built schools.

But the United States soon lost its enthusiasm for annexing this troubled island and decided that it only wanted to be able to control it from a distance. So in 1901, the United States nurtured a new constitution for Cuba: it was to be a democratic republic with universal suffrage, the separation of church and state, and a directly elected president. But there was a catch, in the form of a series of restrictions drafted by then–U.S. Secretary of War Elihu Root. These restrictions barred Cuba from signing treaties that impaired its sovereignty or contracted unpayable debt, and stipulated that the U.S. military had the right to intervene in Cuban affairs anytime it saw fit. Cuba's Constitutional Assembly tried to revise these terms, but the United States informed them that there was to be no revision and that the terms, known as the Platt Amendment, were to be a permanent part of the Cuban constitution. Otherwise, the U.S. military would not leave. Furthermore, the United States had the right to maintain a naval station in Guantánamo for the next eighty years.

The Cubans finally got the Platt Amendment repealed in 1934, but they are still trying to negotiate the withdrawal of the U.S. Navy from Guantánamo.

In the decades that followed, Cuba struggled with democratic elections, which sometimes led to dictatorships, popular uprisings, and even armed rebellion—constant new beginnings. The United States did not see fit to foster the democratic ideals it had professed. When Cuba's struggling experiments with democracy ended with a coup d'état by Fulgencio Batista in 1952, the Americans supported him and even sent him weapons and equipment. They reasoned that at least this was a man with whom they could do business, even though most of Batista's business involved enriching himself, mainly by means of his connections with American organized crime.

Cubans love symbolism. When Fidel Castro and his revolutionaries overthrew Batista, they consciously took Havana on January 1, 1959, sixty years to the day after the United States had taken over.

SEVEN

The Death It Has Given Us

Quieren que esa muerte que nos han regalado
sea la fuente de nuestro nacimiento.

They want that death they have given us as a gift
to be the source of our birth.

— José Lezama Lima, "Pensamientos en La Habana" (1944)

WHEN THE UNITED States took over Cuba in 1898, it was essentially extending a relationship that was already in place. American commercial interests had played an important role in the Cuban economy even when the island was a Spanish colony, as Trollope observed on his 1859 visit:

The trade of the country is falling into the hands of foreigners—into those principally of Americans from the States. Havana will soon become as much American as New Orleans.

The connection had begun after the American Revolution, when the British cut off the United States from trade with British colonies, and Cuba replaced Jamaica as a source of tropical products. Soon Americans became heavily invested in sugar, a mainstay of the Cuban economy, and began owning and operating sugar plantations, as well as tobacco plantations, cattle ranches, and mines. This meant that Americans—and not only the Southerners—were also deeply involved in Cuban slavery.

It was American sugar interests that developed the island. Americans built the first railroad in Cuba, in 1837, to connect the sugar producers in the countryside to the port of Havana. Cuba was only the third country in the world to have train service.

Americans also brought steamship service, not only between Havana and the United States but also between Havana and Matanzas and other cities on Cuba's north coast. Americans ran and operated both the steamships and the railroads.

In 1851, the telegraph was introduced by Samuel Kennedy, a New Yorker; it had been introduced in the United States only five years earlier. And it may have been in Cuba that the telephone was actually invented. Antonio Meucci, an Italian living in Havana, devised one in 1871, three years ahead of Alexander Graham Bell.

By the mid-nineteenth century, American tourists were visiting Cuba, and they tried to own this burgeoning business as well, establishing American-owned hotels with names such as the American Hotel and the Havana House. But it was not until the U.S. military occupation of 1898 that Havana became, in the words of the *New York Times*, "over-run with Americans of all ages" wanting to see what Trumbull White had called "our new possession."

A U.S. citizen did not even need a passport to go to Cuba. Some stayed a few weeks, some a few days, and some, known as *patos de la Florida* (after the wood duck, which travels from Florida to Cuba to nest in palm trees), only a few hours before they got back on their boats.

Havana had always enjoyed a high level of sophistication and standard of living compared with other Latin American cities, and was certainly always far ahead of other Caribbean ones. Its streets had lighting beginning in 1768, and it was one of the first Caribbean cities to publish a newspaper, the *Gaʒeta de La Havana*, in 1782.

But by the late 1800s, after a century of political upheavals, the city had fallen into poor repair, and the new American tourists saw it as a backward place where bargains were to be had. Land was cheap, and American real estate companies began buying it up to sell it off at what was to the Cubans an alarming rate. Vedado, the area past central Havana that had only recently been developed, with luxurious gardened homes for the rich, became inundated with Americans snatching up lots and houses at prices they found astoundingly low.

Martí had been right in his prediction that the Americans to the north would exhibit "scorn for us and our ways." The Americans viewed Havana as a decaying slum that U.S. know-how could fix up. Cubans could be fixed up, too, and taught how to look like their northern neighbors. As *Terry's Guide to Cuba* in 1927 observed:

> The present-day Cuban is rapidly becoming American-ized (*americaniɀado*). Thousands act, think, talk, and look like Americans; wear American clothes, ride in Amer. autos; use Amer. furniture and machinery; often time send their children to Amer. colleges; live for a time in the States themselves, or expect to, and eat much Amer. food.

Of course, there is an historical irony here. Terry was only talking about a certain class of Cubans, most from Havana. And after 1959, when Fidel Castro started trying to change this American-built, not to mention American-controlled, society, they were the ones with the most to lose, and the first to leave. By the mid-1970s there weren't many Americanized Cubans left in Havana.

•

TO THE AMERICANS, Havana was just sitting there, waiting for them. As Trumbull White wrote in 1898, "The multi-plication of Americans in the island will of itself correct that which has been its greatest disadvantage from our own point of view, the absence of a congenial American society."

In 1900, private U.S. companies funded by the U.S. government began spending millions of dollars on major projects to make Havana more suitable for Americans. They paved and patched up streets, improved plumbing, introduced the first flush toilets, built new electric plants, wired homes for electricity, brought streetlights to more neighborhoods, and built walkways and fountains in city parks.

The Havana Electric Railway Company, headquartered in New York, built fifteen miles of electric trolley service connecting central Havana with what were then thought of as the suburbs but later became part of the city—Vedado to the west, Cerro and Jesús del Monte to the south of Vedado, and Guanabacoa, celebrated for its mineral springs and health baths, to the east.

More than anything else, it was this New York trolley company that changed the shape of Havana after the U.S. occupation began. Suddenly, the population of a large area had easy access to central Havana. Land was available, and homes could be built with yards and gardens, indoor toilets that flushed, hot and cold water, and electricity. Such homes were not even tremendously expensive, and for anyone with some money who was not a staunch traditionalist, the spacious outlying area had more to offer than Centro Habana and Habana Vieja.

The Americans also brought with them innovations in construction techniques, opening up the city to new architectural possibilities. By the beginning of the twentieth century, the ornate Beaux Arts design that was in vogue in Paris and New York started to appear, followed by art deco and other styles.

By the late twenties, the Almendares River was no longer the western limit of Havana. Across a new bridge—today it is a tunnel—there were the seaside communities of Miramar and Marianao, featuring a golf course, country club, racetrack, casino, and attractive beach. These communities became the favorite new neighborhoods of Americans and are still favorites with foreigners.

Tourism grew steadily in the first half of the twentieth century. In 1912, oil executive Henry Flagler extended his Florida East Coast Railway from Biscayne Bay to Key West. At the time, Key West was the most populous city in South Florida, but Flagler's real interest was to establish a base for trade with nearby Cuba. Train service through Florida to Key West brought Cuba closer to the United States than it had ever been. Havana hosted conventions and was a popular destination for celebrities—as well as for sailors, thanks to the presence of the U.S. Navy at Guantánamo.

When the U.S. occupation began, there were two hundred registered brothels in Havana, and this long-standing Havana trade now grew dramatically. By the early 1930s, more than seven thousand prostitutes were working in the city. For many men, a visit to a prostitute was one of the celebrated features of a trip to Havana, along with music, rum, and cigars.

Innumerable new bars, cafés, and restaurants also sprang up. Havana had always been a town of bars, cafés, and restaurants, but these new establishments were specifically for Americans—Harry's New York Bar, the Texas Bar, the Chicago Restaurant, the Manhattan Café. They would advertise "American cooking," and sometimes "American service," which probably meant fast service, as compared with the usual Cuban pace, which even Cubans sometimes found too slow. (Cubans aren't slow anymore. One of the messages of the revolution is that hard work is a revolutionary act, and this message and the new status of service jobs in the tourist industry have led to industrious and efficient workers. If you look around Havana today, not a lot of loafing is seen among people on the job, despite the heat.)

Stores began to specialize in American food, medicine, soap, clothes, and other products. Cubans selling Cuban products also sometimes gave their stores American names. And even in Spanish, food stores became known as "groceries." Careers were made by representing or distributing American goods or by serving as an attorney for U.S. companies.

Extraordinarily, in a country famous for its own tobacco products, American cigarettes became fashionable. American automobile companies, especially Ford, established local dealerships. *Un Ford* came to mean a taxi, though today a taxi is more commonly called *un Chevy*. By 1930 there were more cars per capita in Havana than in New York City.

Pets in Havana quite often had, and still have, American names, and they learn basic commands in English.

Habaneros are animal lovers, and Havana is a city of cats and dogs, even though it is poor and has food shortages at times. It is easy to see by the way animals act here that they are rarely mistreated. The cats are lean but friendly, exactly like the people.

Christmas became completely Americanized and began to be celebrated on December 25 instead of January 6, the traditional Día de los Reyes. And Santa Claus arrived. Affluent families began celebrating on both the 25th and the 6th. In the past half-century, the revolution has been struggling to expel Santa Claus, but Habaneros still celebrate the American Christmas, along with such American holidays as Mother's Day and Father's Day.

In 1921, Havana became one of the first cities in the world to have an international airport. The first regular flights were from Key West, via Aeromarine Airways. Pan Am began flying to Havana in 1928, and by the 1930s numerous airlines offered flights to Havana from several American cities.

Also among the firsts that America brought to Havana were some of the world's first theaters to play talkie movies. In 1950, Havana became the first Latin American country to have television, and in 1958, the first to have color TV. At the time of the 1959 revolution, 138 movie theaters were operating in Havana.

Numerous Havana companies did a brisk business in glossy black-and-white publicity photographs of Hollywood stars. Habaneros liked to place these in shops, restaurants, and private homes, and after the revolution they did the same with glossies of Fidel and Che—a tradition that continues today.

Habaneros have always loved movie stars, and it was not incidental to the popularity of the revolution that it was carried out by men who looked like movie stars. Havana literature makes constant references to Hollywood films. Nothing could be more Habanero than Leonardo Padura's 2005 mystery novel *Adiós Hemingway*, which is centered around the fact—at least everyone in Havana says it is a fact—that Ava Gardner swam naked in Hemingway's swimming pool. There is a murder involved, and naturally a key piece of evidence is the lace panties Ms. Gardner discarded before the plunge.

Along the Prado and Parque Central were elegant hotels such as the nineteenth-century Inglaterra and the 1908 Sevilla, built in Moorish Revival style with lacy white railings and fairy-tale turquoise archways. In 1924, when Havana was still a mostly two-story city, a ten-story modern wing was added to the hotel, with a rooftop ballroom built by the celebrated New York architectural firm Schultze and Weaver. After American organized crime started to take over Havana tourism in the 1950s, the Sevilla, by then the Sevilla Biltmore, was part-owned by the infamous Santo Trafficante Jr., who moved to Havana in 1950 to avoid prosecution in Florida.

As Havana expanded into Vedado in 1930, a leading hotel, Hotel Nacional, was built on the Vedado waterfront.

It was designed by the New York firm McKim, Mead and White, known for its many celebrated buildings in New York City, such as the Columbia University campus, the original Pennsylvania Station, and the Morgan Library, as well as the Boston Public Library and the National Museum of Natural History, in Washington. For the Nacional, the firm turned to the Mediterranean Revival style that had become popular with the wealthy people brought to Florida by Flagler's railroad. The new Vedado hotel resembled the already famous Breakers Hotel, in Palm Beach, which had been rebuilt in 1925 by Schultze and Weaver. The Nacional was Havana's largest hotel, with five hundred rooms, and was the first to overlook the ocean.

The Americans were rebuilding Havana in their own image. And if American tastes leaned toward Jim Crow, so be it—anything to please Americans. Poet Nicolás Guillén wrote about watching a couple trying to check in at the Nacional. A white man accompanied by a young black woman was being told that there was absolutely no room available for them in the large hotel. It made no difference that the woman happened to be the celebrated entertainer Josephine Baker, in the city for a performance. They went to another hotel, smaller and less popular with Americans. Guillén wrote, "The Hotel Nacional is Yankee Territory. In Havana it stands for pieces of Virginia or Georgia, places where to be black is barely a humanized form of being a dog." Then came the perfectly tuned Habanero sarcasm. "Having said that, let us be fair: it must be noted that at no time did Mrs. Baker run the risk of being lynched as she would have in Richmond or Atlanta. Is this not a clear sign of progress for which we Cubans should be proud of ourselves?"

Havana's skyline was now marked not only by the Spanish Morro but by the twin towers of the Nacional and by one other facade, the large white dome of El Capitolio, the capitol, home of the legislature of the struggling Cuban republic. The building was completed in 1929 under Gerardo Machado, the democratically elected president, who, after a brief flirtation with democracy, decided that autocracy worked better; he was eventually violently overthrown. Though Machado did not leave democratic institutions in his wake, he did leave this very large legislative building—larger than the one in Washington, D.C., of which it appears to be a copy, despite official denials. The floor under the capitol dome is supposedly a diamond-encrusted rock, from which distances between the capital and all points in Cuba are measured. The estimated cost of the building was twenty million dollars, and it was said to have bankrupted the national treasury.

Like a French president, Machado was determined to leave his visual mark on the city, and in addition to El Capitolio he built the Malecón, a boulevard that runs along the Atlantic seawall in Vedado. For centuries, the seafront there had been a kind of no-man's-land, with rogue waves unpredictably smashing into the rocks and splashing up onto the land. Parts of the waterfront had been a garbage dump during the last years of Spanish rule. But in 1902, during the U.S. occupation, General Wood had a seawall built, and later, when cars began appearing in significant numbers in Havana, a scenic drive was constructed alongside it. Under Machado in 1930, that drive was extended to run along the entire curved waterfront of Vedado—a seven-mile sweep from Habana Vieja to the Almendares River.

The Malecón completely changed Havana's perspective. Until its construction, Havana was a city on the bay. Once the Malecón was built, Habaneros turned their heads from the bay to the ocean. Havana became a city on the sea, on the Atlantic, the Straits, facing the Gulf Stream— the city to which Hemingway was drawn. The Malecón is still a favorite spot—the place to go fishing, the place for lovers to walk along while listening to a rumbling sea or to embrace in the shadows, the place to pick out a tune on a guitar at night, the only place in Havana with Atlantic breezes on a relentlessly broiling day, the place to cool off at nighttime, the place to take refuge behind the endless columns of the buildings along the boulevard, the place to face the sea where the ocean runs a bit wild and whitecaps lap and splash over the edge of the road. It was thrilling to drive past the waves. As Cabrera Infante wrote in his novel *Three Trapped Tigers*, "I'm only saying for the benefit of those who have never traveled in a convertible along the Malecón between five and seven in the afternoon or rather evening on August 11, 1958, at sixty or eighty miles an hour: such privilege, such exaltation, such euphoria . . ."

For Havana children, there is no greater joy on a hot day, which is almost every day, than running in the waves that splash over the Malecón. Everyone who has grown up in Havana has childhood memories of the Malecón. Carlos Eire, the privileged son of a Batista-era judge, in his reminiscences of his childhood, *Waiting for Snow in Havana*, described persuading his father to drive through the waves along the Malecón when a storm came.

An entire volume could be collected of poetry about the Malecón—from Ibarzábal's "Noche Habanero" to Bernard Jambrina's "En el Malecón" to Agustín Acosta's "En el Malecón" to Carpentier's "Las Tardes del Malecón," and many, many more.

Adding to the boulevard's romance is a vague but titillating whiff of danger. The sea heaves, seems to show its muscles, and crashes against the wall, spraying the road. Then waves actually rise up over the wall and splash across the road, with foam marking the points of contact, sometimes even wrapping around the pillars of the buildings on the far side of the boulevard. This is when the thought intrudes, *How serious could this get?*

Very serious. The word "hurricane" comes from the Taino language, and the Tainos drew spirals to symbolize it. Havana is hurricane country. The most damaging hurricane ever recorded—there may well have been worse ones that were recorded only by those Taino spirals—was the Hurricane of Santa Teresa on October 15, 1768. There was no way to measure wind velocity back then, but entire blocks were torn to rubble, and the inner harbor, which was supposed to be safe, was invaded by a furious sea that, when it withdrew, carried away all the anchored ships. In 2005, another October storm, Hurricane Wilma, came in through the Malecón and immersed much of the city in three and four feet of seawater. Although 130,000 people were evacuated and large hunks of the Malecón ripped out and washed away, leaving the seaward side of the already half-ruined Vedado looking a little worse, there were no fatalities. The Malecón was easily repaired, and little permanent damage was done to the old, rickety city, perhaps because it was a wreck to begin with.

•

PROHIBITION, THE CONSTITUTIONAL banning of alcoholic beverages in the United States between 1920 and 1933, offered a new opportunity for Havana. This was the original attraction of organized crime to Havana. Cuban establishments that catered to Americans could now offer them the drinks they couldn't have at home. President Machado must have delighted in having a waiter bring Calvin Coolidge a daiquiri with the press watching during the U.S. president's 1928 visit. The press, for its part, was impressed with how artfully Coolidge managed to have Machado's attention drawn elsewhere while he evaded the waiter and the drink.

But most Americans not only didn't decline the proffered libations—they came to Havana to drink. Even without organized crime, this was a great business for Havana bars. Probably the most famous, near the Sevilla Biltmore, was Sloppy Joe's, housed in a large space with a long, dark mahogany bar and many tall, dark wooden tables and mirrors. It had as its slogan "First port of call, out where the wet begins."

This is the bar where Carol Reed shot the scene in *Our Man in Havana* where the vacuum cleaner salesman is recruited by British intelligence. Such things may have happened there. It looked like it, anyway, in this large bar crowded almost entirely with foreigners.

A Spaniard, José Abeal y Otero, known to his American customers as Sloppy Joe, opened the bar when Prohibition started. According to Abeal, who circulated booklets with the bar's story in the 1930s, it first opened for business inside a grocery store in 1918. Because of the store's disheveled appearance, American customers started calling it "Sloppy Joe's." Another story is that the bar's name came from a negative review.

Sloppy Joe's specialized in a sandwich of the same name that was a perfect expression of Havana at the time. It was the traditional Cuban dish picadillo, served on an American-style hamburger bun.

Below is the recipe as the bartender gave it to me, translated into English. But first you have to make a picadillo, so here is a recipe for picadillo given to me more than thirty years ago at an equally famous Havana bar, La Bodeguita del Medio:

> Grind meat (beef) and marinate it with salt and lime juice, or vinegar. Make a *sofrito* with minced garlic and onion sautéd with the ground meat. This should be done slowly.

Now the Sloppy Joe:

> Saute picadillo in oil: add black pepper, onion, garlic, cumin, bay leaf, and tomato sauce, and finish with demiglace sauce. Add salt to taste and when it is cooked, add (green) olives. Keep on medium heat for 5 minutes to finish. Serve over a hamburger bun.

A "Sloppy Joe's" was also a drink popular in the 1930s, served in a tall glass with crushed ice and a straw. The key to this drink is the high booze-to-fruit-juice ratio. The ingredients, according to the bar's brochure:

> 2 ounces pineapple juice
> 1 ounce cognac
> 1 ounce port wine
> ¼ teaspoon orange curaçao
> ¼ teaspoon grenadine

Sloppy Joe's was famous for cocktails, which were very much a Havana fashion. The bar boasted eighty cocktail recipes, including the American Girl and the Mary Pickford, the latter made of pineapple, rum, and grenadine, a kind of simplified Sloppy Joe's.

Iced drinks were a Cuban specialty in the nineteenth century, when only a few warm places, notably Havana and New Orleans, had ample supplies of ice. The ice came from up north: blocks were harvested in Upstate New York and New England, stored in insulated icehouses, and then shipped from New York and Boston directly to Havana.

Havana first got ice in 1806, and in *Cecilia Valdés*, the white planter class sips away the hot afternoons with iced drinks. In 1871, Samuel Hazard was surprised at how readily available ice was in Havana. Street carts selling snow cones—shaved ice with a large choice of syrups— were common in Centro Habana from the nineteenth century until 1959, when the revolution abolished private business.

The cuba libre was one of the first of the famous Cuban iced cocktails. American soldiers, the Rough Riders, brought Coca-Cola to Cuba and soon started spiking it with rum, often toasting to a "free Cuba," the cause for which they claimed to be fighting. Soon the recipe became Habanero, with a splash of lime juice added and sometimes a splash of bitters, served in a tall glass of ice.

Another famed Havana bar, El Floridita, was founded in 1912 by Constantino "Constante" Ribalaigua, a small man reputed to be a great bartender and to have perfected the daiquiri—in part by adding maraschino liqueur to the formula. Like the cuba libre, the daiquiri was invented in eastern Cuba, but improved upon in Havana. Daiquirí is the name of a mining town in eastern Cuba, and supposedly an American mining engineer named Jennings Cox concocted the original drink—essentially rum, lime juice, sugar, and ice—when he ran out of gin. Others say it was not Cox, but an American soldier, William Shafter, who invented the daiquiri in Santiago when he added ice to a local lime-and-rum drink. In either case, ice was the pivotal ingredient for an American cocktail.

Originally, El Floridita had huge open doorways to let in air, and big, thumping ceiling fans. Its crowd spread out onto the street. Hemingway could leave his hotel, walk past the shops on Calle Obispo, catering mostly to Americans, then cool off with an iced drink at El Floridita. It was a good life.

•

A *BODEGUITA* IS a small bodega, a little grocery store, usually equipped with a bar. Ángel Martínez started one in 1942. It was supposed to be named Casa Martínez, but everyone called it La Bodeguita del Medio—the little bodega halfway down the block. In 1951, he partnered with Sepy Dobronyi, a Hungarian who had been everything from a pilot to a jewelry designer to a painter, and La Bodeguita was reinvented as a bar and restaurant. The concept, perfect for Havana, was slum chic. Here movie stars such as Errol Flynn could drink and dine cheaply on peasant fare in a series of small rooms of tawdry charm while listening to well-played songs: boleros and the peasant songs known as guajiras. Customers were encouraged to cover the walls with their graffiti.

Among the Cuban peasant dishes served in La Bodeguita was ajiaco. Though central to Havana cooking, it is of rural origin, from the sugar plantations, where root vegetables provided slaves with inexpensive nutrition. Alfonso Hernández Catá, Cuba's first great short story writer, from the early twentieth century, wrote a story about a veteran telling his children a tale from the War of Independence. Before he tells it to them, he insists they eat ajiaco. It is a way to be in touch with *cubanismo*.

Ajiaco is considered to be the quintessential Cuban dish because it includes indigenous roots such as yucca, known as cassava in English; boniato, a white sweet potato; and malanga, a root that is similar to taro. African products such as yams and plantains; and European meats. On one of the marked-up blue walls of La Bodeguita, someone has written: YO MI APETITO SOLO APLACA EN LA MESA EN QUE BRILLA UN BUEN AJIACO—My appetite is aroused only by a table that shines with a good ajiaco.

This is La Bodeguita's recipe:

In a casserole dish, cover salt beef, strips of pork, beef, and bacon with water. Bring this to a boil and add two or three very ripe plátanos, boniato, malanga, cassava, chayote, eggplant, an ear of sweet corn, pumpkin squash, and, if you want, some potatoes too. Let it boil for an hour. Grind spices in a mortar, add some saffron, and mix with some of the stock from the casserole. Add to the casserole. Add a little bit of lime juice and boil for another fifteen minutes.

The drink that La Bodeguita became famous for was the mojito. This cocktail, made popular by Ángel Martínez, is now associated with Havana, but its origin is uncertain and might trace back centuries. While daiquiris are poured into glasses filled with crushed ice, mojitos have only a few cubes, which suggests that it is an older drink.

To me, the mojito is *the* taste of Havana. I arrive, I sip my first mojito, and I know I am in Havana. This is partly because it used to be that you found mojitos nowhere else. Now they are everywhere—in New York, Paris, and Tokyo. But none of these impostors taste like the true mojito, because their preparation involves a fatal mistake: the wrong kind of mint. A mojito has to be made with the tropical spearmint that grows in Cuba, which they call *yerba buena*. To be honest, my feeling for the drink may be excessive; at one point in the 1980s, the government official in charge of monitoring me actually nicknamed me "Mojito."

This is La Bodeguita's recipe:

Mix ½ tablespoon of sugar and the juice of half a lime in a highball glass. Add spearmint leaves and crush them to release the juice. Add two ice cubes and 1½ ounces of Havana Club Light Dry (rum). Fill to the top with soda water and stir.

Although the above recipe calls for granulated sugar, I have noticed that at La Bodeguita they use cane syrup, which is a much better way to mix the drink. Some Havana bars also add a splash of angostura bitters, which is also a good idea.

•

WHEN BATISTA CAME to power, first in 1940 and especially the second time, after a coup in 1952, he realized that the more and bigger the projects he was involved in, the more money was available for him to steal, and so he offered government money, tax breaks, and subsidies for construction projects, all of which attracted American investors. Some of these investors were organized crime figures such as Santo Trafficante and Meyer Lansky.

In 1946, a kind of superpower summit of the underworld was convened at the Hotel Nacional. Lucky Luciano, the man credited with organizing crime in the United States, had been deported and was attempting to live in Havana. But he was about to be forced back to his native Sicily, and the purpose of the meeting was to appoint a boss to run the gambling syndicate that controlled many of Havana's casinos. Numerous members of New York crime families were there, as well as Joe and Rocco Fischetti, from Al

Capone's Chicago organization, accompanied by singer Frank Sinatra. In the end it was Meyer Lansky, whom Luciano had known since childhood on the Lower East Side of New York, who was officially pronounced the boss of Cuban gambling.

Both gambling and government payoffs from gambling are time-honored traditions in Havana. In *Cecilia Valdés*, Villaverde says that in the early nineteenth century, "gaming houses in Cuba paid a contribution to the government for supposedly charitable causes."

•

IN THE 1950S, hundreds more bars and nightclubs opened near the Prado and Vedado around Calle 23, which is still a lively area; it's called La Rampa because it is built on a slight hill. Nightclubs also started opening beyond Vedado. The Sans Souci, just outside of town, created the illusion of a country estate, with gardens to stroll through and open-air dancing to famous bands. International performers ranging from Edith Piaf to Harry Belafonte to Marlene Dietrich to Sarah Vaughn, as well as Cuban stars such as Benny Moré, the great bolero singer, performed there. Meyer Lansky operated the casino.

Also in the suburbs just outside Marianao was the Tropicana, with its spectacular 1940s architecture, notably Max Borges's Arcos de Cristal—huge concrete arches with glass walls. The Tropicana is the only one of the famous clubs from that era to survive and has been operated for all

these years by the revolutionary government. It looks a little threadbare and is completely out of place in revolutionary Havana—Cubans don't go there—but the architecture
is still stunning, and, of course, despite the official position
of the revolutionary government against the peddling of
flesh, the women are still beautiful and nearly naked.

Graham Greene, in describing his trips to Havana in his
autobiography, *Ways of Escape*, may have expressed what
other men thought, only with a great deal more candor:

> I enjoyed the louche atmosphere of Batista's city and I
> never stayed long enough to become aware of the sad
> political background of arbitrary imprisonment and
> torture. I came there . . . for the sake of the Floridita

Backstage at the Tropicana, July 1982. Photograph by Maggie
Steber.

restaurant (famous for daiquiris and Morro crabs), for the brothel life, the roulette in every hotel, the fruit machines spilling out jackpots of silver dollars, the Shanghai Theater where for one dollar and twenty-five cents one could see a nude cabaret of extreme obscenity with the bluest of blue films in the intervals.

He described an evening with a friend at the Shanghai watching a character called Superman having sex with a mulata—but complained that Superman's performance was as "uninspiring as a dutiful husband's"—before going on to lose a little money at roulette, eat dinner at El Floridita, smoke a little marijuana, and see a lesbian show at the Blue Moon. All this was followed by their driver scoring them a little cocaine for an incredibly cheap price from a news-stand. The dealer turned out to be crooked, the cocaine just white powder. It was after such an evening that Greene was inspired to move his spy comedy, later to be titled *Our Man in Havana*, from Europe to Havana. "Suddenly it struck me that here in this extraordinary city, where every vice was permissible and every trade possible, lay the true back-ground for my comedy." For better or worse, probably both, all this ended with the revolution.

In the late 1950s, Havana saw the beginning of what in other beachfront cities became a wall of high-rise concrete hotels. In 1955, Meyer Lansky began his dream of building the most luxurious beachfront hotel in the Caribbean—the Habana Riviera, in Vedado. Lansky built it with his own money, money from Las Vegas investors, and six million dollars in government loans from his friend Batista. It was a twenty-one-story hotel designed by Igor Polevitzky, who, with such buildings as the 1940 Shelborne Hotel, was a leading influence in Miami Beach's high-rise beachfront. Among the prominent attractions of the Riviera was that it was the first building in Havana to have central air conditioning, still a rare feature in the city.

The Havana Hilton, which opened in 1958, was a thirty-story building at the edge of La Rampa, in Vedado, and was visible from anywhere in the city, its owners boasted. It had 630 rooms, a large swimming pool, a casino, and a rooftop lounge, which, as the old joke goes, had the best view in Havana because you didn't see the Hilton.

Though it infuriates opponents of the revolution, the argument can be and often is made that the revolution saved Havana. It saved it from becoming Miami Beach or San Juan, Puerto Rico. It saved the Malecón from being sealed off from the rest of the city by high-rise hotels. And it saved Havana from Josep Lluís Sert and his Harvard-trained, Le Corbusier–influenced architects, who had submitted to the city a proposal to modernize Havana. The antique buildings of Habana Vieja were to be replaced by concrete and glass, the narrow streets widened and paved to be more suitable for car traffic, and the ancient Spanish plazas turned into parking lots. Sert was planning for a population of four million, twice the size of Havana today.

Castro saw how other Latin American cities, such as Santo Domingo, Mexico City, and Caracas, were becoming overwhelmed by migrants from the countryside looking for opportunities that, in many cases, weren't there. He instituted laws so that in revolutionary Cuba, a Cuban wishing to move to the capital has to apply and show a well-organized plan for a successful life there. Havana is not for all Cubans.

EIGHT

The Twenty-Six-Flavor Revolution

Esta ciudad picante y loca . . .

This city, piquant and crazy . . .

— FEDERICO DE IBARZÁBAL, "Una Ciudad del Trópico" (1919)

WHEN I FIRST got to Havana in the early 1980s, I stayed at the Havana Hilton, which by then was called the Habana Libre. I didn't choose to stay there; it was where the Cuban government put American journalists. While I was appreciative of the air conditioning, and didn't mind the lack of a casino, the place seemed antiseptic in a city that was just the opposite. Also, it was hard not to feel controlled. The phones were rumored to be tapped, and the government functionaries with whom journalists were in contact made it clear that they were aware of lunches and other plans that had been discussed over the phone. They seemed more interested in showing off their inside knowledge than in concealing their espionage.

The huge lobby had a lot of bored men sitting around who looked like government agents—one of them always "coincidentally" getting up just as you were leaving. There were also women who appeared to be prostitutes but had some connection to the government agents. It was, after all, a nationalized economy.

Some point out that the revolution started out bloody and ruthless, which is true. But it also started out idealistic and completely impractical. The government did not immediately realize that if you own a high-rise luxury hotel like the Habana Libre, something profitable ought to be done with it. And so the hotel was initially used for the party loyal, thousands of peasants, who were bused in to cheer Fidel at rallies. Housing peasants in the luxury hotel was ideologically pitch-perfect, although the peasants, not accustomed to luxury hotels and billeted several to a room, did not always leave the place in the best condition. In time, the new government realized that this was not a good use of one of its few luxury hotels.

During one trip, after a week in the Habana Libre, I decided to drift on my own to a small hotel in Vedado. My room there was much smaller, and its air conditioner was a noisy box in the window, but there was no lobby for anyone to sleepily sit in.

At the time, there were only two television channels in Cuba. One was a political channel with the official line on everything; it was somewhat helpful to journalists. The other was a cultural channel, and I found myself wanting to stay in some nights for the great Cuban movies on television.

During that trip, I saw *Memorias del Subdesarollo* (*Memories of Underdevelopment*), Tomás Gutiérrez Alea's classic 1968 black-and-white film of Edmundo Desnoes's

1965 novel *Inconsolable Memories*—one of the first novels written about life in revolutionary Cuba—about a man lost in the revolution after everyone he knows has left for Miami. There were two other great Gutiérrez films: *La Muerte de un Burócrata* (*Death of a Bureaucrat*), a very dark and funny 1966 comedy about the bureaucracy of the revolution, and *La Ultima Cena* (*The Last Supper*), a spellbinding historical drama about an eighteenth-century planter who invites twelve of his slaves to a dinner to reenact the Last Supper.

Night after night, my TV offered brilliant films I had never heard of—films criticizing the government and talking about sexism, racism, and materialism. It was, and is, an unresolvable contradiction that this police state manages social criticism so well. In 1993, Gutiérrez and Carlos Tabío made *Fresa y Chocolate* (*Strawberry and Chocolate*), criticizing the homophobia of the government. Most of the foreign press wrote about this film as though it had been made in courageous defiance of the government, but it was a government-sponsored film.

Three facts: Cubans talk a lot, Cuban politicians talk even more, and Fidel Castro broke all records. One night in my small room with the noisy air conditioner, I decided to conscientiously listen to a speech being broadcast by Fidel Castro. He was said to have had a photographic memory, and that night he spoke extemporaneously for hours. I fell asleep. Suddenly there was an abrupt pounding on the door. I opened my eyes and stumbled over to open it.

A man in a uniform handed me a notice on the low-quality paper the government always used. He was wearing the greenish uniform of MININT, the security service of the Ministry of the Interior.

My first reaction was one of awe. How did they know I had fallen asleep on Fidel? The piece of paper ordered me, in extremely rude language—Cuban authorities are generally very polite to American journalists—to report to the ministry at ten the following morning. I quickly realized that this was not about falling asleep on Fidel, but I never found out what it was about. When I arrived at the ministry the next morning, a polite man in uniform asked to see my return ticket. As it happened, I was leaving the next day. He shook my hand warmly and wished me a good flight.

·

IF I SEEMED paranoid, and if revolutionary Havana seems like a paranoid society, it was—and is—but not without reason. Assaults from the sea remain a fear in the culture, for after the pirates, the British, and the Spanish troops came and went, the Americans arrived—to take over "the independence."

In 1961, the CIA and Cuban exiles tried to invade the island. The United States was feeling threatened by Cuba's increasingly Communist revolutionary government, and the exiled anti-Castro Cubans had assured the CIA— erroneously, as it turned out—that the Cubans were ready to rise up and overthrow Castro. The main invading force landed at the Bay of Pigs, on the southern coast, coming ashore on a beautiful, isolated, rock-studded white-sand beach called Playa Girón. They were defeated in three days by the Cuban Revolutionary Army.

Another confrontation between Cuba and the United States occurred the next year, when John F. Kennedy confronted the Soviet Union over missile deployment in Cuba. Havana and the rest of the island braced themselves for another invasion, but the crisis was averted and the invasion never happened.

Thereafter, Havana—as well as the rest of the island—remained vigilant. Sandbags, antiaircraft guns, and militiamen filled the city's waterfront, the Malecón. Even matchbooks, a state concession like almost everything else after the revolution, for decades had printed on them *"Ciudad de La Habana listos para la defense"*—"The city of Havana prepared for defense."

Desnoes, in the novel *Inconsolable Memories*, re-creates that time: Fidel had said, "Everybody, young and old, men and women, we are all one in this hour of danger!" But, far from being inspired, Desnoes's character thinks, "We're all one, I'll die like everybody else. This island is a trap and the revolution is tragic because we're too small to survive, to come through. Too poor and too few."

Cuba's paranoia proved to be permanent, and was fueled, as it often is, by reality. The CIA, under Kennedy, launched Operation Mongoose, a program of dirty tricks that included assassination attempts as well as sabotage.

Remembering how, centuries earlier, pirates had sent friendly visitors into Havana to gather information about the harbor and its fortifications so that they could report back to their ship and attack, the government for decades after the revolution forbade anyone from shooting photographs of the harbor. If a tourist or journalist so much as held up a camera in the vicinity of the waterfront, an official was on hand to intervene.

This kind of paranoia has few boundaries. In Antonio Benítez Rojo's 1967 short story "Buried Statues," the narrator suggests, and his mother agrees, that butterflies "were some secret weapon that we didn't understand yet."

And yet, who can say what was, or is, real? The CIA always denied the story that Operation Mongoose had included plans to assassinate Castro with an exploding cigar. But the U.S. Senate's Church Committee, which investigated CIA excess in 1975, identified eight separate attempts on Fidel Castro's life. They could not confirm the exploding cigar, but poisoned cigars intended for the Cuban leader were sent to Cuba, and there was a plot to slip a depilatory into his shoes to cause his beard and eyebrows to fall out. If the depilatories stuffed in shoes and the poisoned cigars were real, who can say with certitude what butterflies are up to? Or what else might be coming from across the sea?

A system of neighborhood snitching is extensive in Cuba. It is called the Committees for the Defense of the Revolution (CDR) and is founded on the same idea as the "If you see something, say something" campaign against terrorism in the United States.

The Cubans may have over-organized. There are fifteen thousand committees in Havana, and one hundred thousand throughout the island. Many of the people doing this work are nothing more than neighborhood gossips inundating the intelligence service, G2, with trivia. Gossip has always been a way of life in Havana. People know that what they do and say will get reported. Yet Habaneros have grown accustomed to this and don't seem to speak particularly carefully.

The CDR is also involved in neighborhood services such as day care and community health initiatives. It is part of a government that is extremely good, for better and worse, at organizing people. The CDR has managed to guarantee that there is at least one working doctor on every block in Havana.

•

WHEN FIDEL CASTRO was Cuba's leader, every May 1—May Day, the traditional holiday of world socialism—a huge rally was held in the sprawling trapezoid-shaped Plaza de la Revolución, at the southern end of Vedado. Built by Batista, who had named it Plaza Cívica, it contains a tall obelisk that appears to have fins running up its side like a great white sea monster rising straight out of the plaza. Nearby is a white marble statue of José Martí, who seems to be squatting uncomfortably.

On May 1, Fidel would march out onto the platform to deliver his speech. When he was younger, he was a very large, powerfully built, and athletic man with a virile charisma, a kind of electricity that I have seen fill large rooms and that even pulsated through this enormous plaza.

I attended a number of these May Day events. The government wanted foreign journalists to cover them, so it was an easy time to get a press visa. The plaza was always full, because these were events for which people from the countryside were bused in. They were now housed in dormitories rather than the luxurious Habana Libre, but they still showed the enthusiasm of home team fans at a World Series.

The people carried various symbolic props. In 1985, they had a huge shoe, perhaps twelve feet long, that was paraded around. By then, after two decades of struggling for shoes, and constantly repairing old ones, even sneakers, Cuba was finally manufacturing enough shoes to meet the needs of its people. It was, as the government liked to say, "achieving shoe self-sufficiency."

One of the big problems, especially in Havana, immediately after the revolution and the U.S. trade embargo, had been how to replace American products in a society that had been completely dependent on them. People struggled to find basics like soap and shoes.

Then the Soviet Union stepped in to fill the void. Essentially subsidizing the revolution, it became the island's source of foreign goods. The Cubans had no money during those heady days, and no one was getting rich, but, step by step, problems were being solved with the help of the Russians, and it felt as though the revolution was working.

In time, the Cubans learned how to make many of the things they needed, even baseballs. One of the first problems they solved was how to produce a local Coca-Cola substitute. After all, how were they to drink cuba libres in Cuba Libre without cola? They figured out a formula, but then there was another momentary crisis because, while they could now produce enough cola, they didn't have enough cork for the thin piece that seals the inside of the bottle cap. Soon that problem was solved too, and at the rallies, stands distributed free bottles of Tropi-Cola. In time the government, with the help of Nestlé, produced a similar cola, named TuKola because of the Havana street vendors who'd shout, *"Compre tu cola"*—"Get your Cola." Today the government even exports Tropi-Cola.

Even after solving the cola problem, cuba libres were still in trouble. There was the problem of rum: the island's principal rum makers, including Bacardi, had left. But then the Bacardi distillery at Santiago became nationalized, and Cubans began producing their own rum. Another leading brand, Havana Club, was owned by the Arechebala family, who had also left. The Cuban government solved that by forming a partnership with Pernod Ricard, the French liquor multinational, to make Havana Club, and the future of cuba libres seemed secured.

Then there was the problem of ice. Once Havana's cocktail trademark, ice had started to become scarce. Only certain bars catering to foreigners had ice, because ice making requires a great deal of electricity and Cubans were being pressured to conserve energy. Leonardo Padura wrote of a character trying to order a daiquiri in a bar, the way Hemingway liked them, with lots of shaved ice and no sugar, only to be sneered at by the bartender: "The last time I saw a piece of ice was when I was a penguin."

•

THE LACK OF new cars and car parts has always been another problem in Cuba, although it is a problem that for all these years has spared Havana from another problem: the traffic congestion that plagues most cities. Perhaps this is why Habaneros habitually walk in the middle of the street, stroll the road on the Malecón. But walking in the middle of the street is also a Havana habit that began long before the revolution. It probably began in Habana Vieja, because the sidewalks there are too narrow for a couple to walk down abreast.

By the 1950s, however, the affluent Habanero family was no longer living in the cramped center of the city, but farther out, and had an automobile—to be precise, an American car. By the end of the decade there were 170,000 cars in

Cuba, almost all American, and most were in Havana. A ridiculously high number of them were Cadillacs, but there were also Buicks, Chryslers, Studebakers, Chevys, Fords—everything people were driving in America.

After the revolution, when an affluent family wanted to leave Cuba, they were required to take their car to a garage for a tune-up and present the car to the government with a certificate that it was in top working order. The government could then give out these cars, many of them late models, to whomever they pleased. Being a good revolutionary came with perks.

Yet the perks also came with challenges. Like the shoe repairmen who had to learn how to rebuild sneakers, Habanero mechanics now had to learn how to keep cars running without parts from their manufacturers. Some solved problems by adapting engine parts from other models. Today many Chevies and other classics run with newer Toyota engines. One mechanic even claimed to have installed a boat engine in a car. Meanwhile, some original engines rumbled and grumbled so loudly that they got the name *cafeteros*—coffee percolators.

But there is a Havana club of vintage car owners who value only cars that are purely, or almost purely, original. There is more to this than just hobbyism. A quality antique car can land its owner a job as a tourist taxi driver, and tourist taxi drivers can earn one of the better incomes in Havana.

During the Soviet era, Ladas came to Cuba. A Lada was a Russian-made car built mostly for export. The cars were designed to endure the rugged conditions of Siberia, and so were thought to be ideal for Cuba's deteriorating roads and streets. Boxy cars that were extremely rigid and uncomfortable, Ladas were almost the exact opposite of the 1950s American cars, with their plush upholstery, spacious seating, and design that emphasized curves. But even worse, Ladas turned out to be not at all durable. A '55 Chevy today is usually in better condition than an '85 Lada.

•

THE DETERIORATING LADAS may be taken as a metaphor for Cuba's entire relationship with the Soviet Union. Little has endured, despite thirty years of intimacy. There must have been some affection for the Russians, though, because Russian names such as Vladimir became fashionable, and many people in Havana born in the sixties, seventies, and eighties have Russian first names. People of that generation also learned to speak Russian, but they seldom speak it now, and most say they can't remember it. Russian style never caught on in this Latin country, either. Though most Habaneros do not have the resources for fine clothes, they do have a sense of fashion, and they found the ill-fitting suits and jeans and baggy dresses and head scarves of the Russians unappealing.

While the Russians contributed to the country economically and in other ways, they seldom spoke Spanish and were seldom integrated into Cuban life. Rather than take a stately old mansion for an embassy, for example, they built a huge, intimidating concrete structure that looked more like a fortress than La Cabaña or the Morro. But the modern design was well suited for surveillance systems, some of which are still visible from the outside.

The Russians shopped, buying vodka and caviar, in their own separate stores, at least one of which still exists, if you know the right people. In 2012, a Cuban chef who had access took me shopping, though he declined to explain why he had access to the Russian store. It seemed like a visit back to the Soviet Union that had disappeared twenty years before. The shop was in a gated compound in Vedado. It seemed to be modeled after an old speakeasy. Each prospective customer would come up to the man at the gate and whisper something, and the gate would open or the customer would be waved away.

Once inside, we found ourselves in a small room with a counter in front of somewhat sparsely stocked shelves, just as in a real Cuban store. There were various European liquors and liqueurs and a few prized Russian products, such as red and black caviars. Prices were more than most Cubans could pay, but not particularly expensive by Western standards. There were also some mundane items like soaps and detergents, many of which, despite the embargo, seemed to be American. For an American, these items did not seem worth bothering with, but for a Cuban they were basics that had disappeared with the embargo.

•

THE REVOLUTION CLOSED the casinos and most clubs and ended private ownership, which meant that stores and restaurants either closed or became state-operated. The suppression of small shops and restaurants drove from Havana two of its important ethnic communities, the Jews and the Chinese, both of whom, like immigrants in most places, were strongly centered around private entrepreneurship.

Jews have a long history in Cuba, and particularly in Havana—especially long if it is true, as is believed, that Columbus's crew included Jews escaping Spanish persecution and passing themselves off as Christians. In Havana, Jews are called *polacos*. Nobody knows why, since the name appears to predate immigration from Poland and the community has always had a large Sephardic component from Brazil and Turkey, among other places. Nobody knows why Americans are called *yumas*, either. Some Americans suggest it is from the 1957 Van Heflin/Glenn Ford film *3:10 to Yuma*, based on an Elmore Leonard story, but I have never met anyone in Havana who has even heard of this movie. Then, too, why are all Spaniards in Cuba called *gallegos*, meaning the people who come from Spain's northwest province of Galicia, when *gallegos* are only one of several Iberian populations on the island? And why are Italians *amicis*? And why is a blonde woman a *negrita*, though she is the opposite? All of these have come about for the same reason: Habaneros love nicknames, and they use them without rancor, prejudice, or logic.

By the 1930s there were twelve thousand Jews in Cuba. Some were American Jews who had fought in the Spanish–American War and stayed. Later, Jews came to escape Hitler.

Jews came but also left. The last rabbi left in 1958, before the revolution. By the time of the revolution, the twelve thousand had grown to only fifteen thousand. There were several synagogues, and Jewish stores and restaurants, which of course were popular with visiting New Yorkers. But after the revolution, most of the remaining Jews, not wishing to have their businesses taken over by the state, left. By the mid-1980s only eight hundred Jews remained in Cuba, most of them in Havana. They still maintained two synagogues, but there was very little religious observance.

Most of the Jews who stayed were secular, and often enthusiastic supporters of the revolution. Among their numbers were Fabio Grobart, a Jewish founder of the Communist Party of Cuba, who used to introduce Castro at party meetings, and Ricardo Subirana y Lobo, who had helped finance Castro's return from exile to begin the revolution.

There is no history of anti-Semitism in Cuba, despite the government's strong anti-Israel stance post-1967 and despite the government's official disdain for organized religion. The government even gives unique privileges to the tiny community, importing special foods such as matzoth for Passover, state-financing religious burials in Havana's Jewish cemetery, and providing extra food rations for Jewish holidays to supplement the basic food rations given to every Cuban.

Once part of the life of Havana, the tiny Jewish community is barely noticed now except by visiting Jews. Young Cuban Jews, like other young Cubans in this very secular society, rarely show interest in traditional religion. Even so, in 1985, one of their leaders, Adela Dworin, who was raised before the revolution as a strictly observant Orthodox Jew, told me, "You can eat pork, you can say, 'I love Communism and hate religion,' but you still feel you are a Jew."

Most of the Chinese also left Havana after the revolution, and today Barrio Chino is just a name, like Vedado. As the last of the restaurants vanished from Chinatown— only two were left in the 1980s—Cuban-Chinese restaurants became a dining trend in New York City.

But the Chinese had a huge impact on Havana life.

In the nineteenth century, as one slaving society after another renounced slavery, Cuban planters looked for an alternative. They brought in Mayan workers from the nearby Yucatán Peninsula of Mexico. The Maya found conditions unbearable and either went back to Mexico or settled in Habana Vieja, in a neighborhood near the wall called Barrio Campeche, after the Mexican state from which they came. Today the neighborhood no longer retains its Mayan character.

The first Chinese workers came to Havana in 1844 from Canton. Conditions on the ships from Asia were barely better than those on the slave ships, and an estimated 12 percent of the Chinese laborers did not survive the passage.

Many had been virtually kidnapped and had no idea where they were going. Upon arrival, they were instantly shipped to plantations, where they worked with African slaves and were kept in similar but separate barracoons. They were forced into eight-year contracts at twenty cents a day, and at the end of their term, if they hadn't died or killed themselves, most returned to China.

But some stayed on the land and worked their own farms; the Chinese are credited with introducing the mango to Cuba. More moved into Centro Habana, to a new neighborhood beyond the wall, and established shops and restaurants. The first Cuban-Chinese restaurant opened in 1858, and many more followed. They created their own cuisine, a natural fusion of two traditions, both strongly rooted in pork and seafood. By the twentieth century, Barrio Chino had become the largest Chinatown in Latin America, with signs in Cantonese and Mandarin, brightly colored paper lanterns, Chinese-language newspapers, and also, this being Havana, prostitution, girlie shows, and gambling.

In Havana, Chinese culture fused easily with Cuban culture, which meant also African culture. One of the most famous Chinese Cubans was the artist Wifredo Lam.

Though born in rural Santa Clara Province, he is often said to be the quintessential Habanero—a man who looked Asian, thanks to a Chinese father, but whose mother was the daughter of an African-born slave and a mulato. Lam was a painter who sought to express the African traditions with which he was raised. He studied in Paris in the 1930s and was greatly influenced by the artists he came to know there, including Breton, Miró, Braque, Léger, and Matisse. He once exhibited in Paris with Picasso. But his work always had African underpinnings.

Another example of the Cuban Afro-Chinese blend is the Chino de la Charada, an illustration that appears to be rooted in Chinese folklore but has overtones of Santería, the West African–derived religion. It is a drawing of a Chinese man in traditional dress carrying a fish in one hand and a pipe in another. His body is covered with images—a butterfly on one ear, a snake on an ankle, a jewel, a chicken, a cat, a skull, a turtle . . . Each image has a number next to it. The drawing was used by the Chinese for numerology-based divination, but others had another use for it—they saw it as a key to what number to play in the lottery. For example, if you saw a butterfly fly by, you could look at the number by the butterfly on La Charada's ear and play that number. Cubans of all ethnicities knew the system. In Graham Greene's autobiography, he tells of a driver in the countryside who accidentally hit a chicken and felt compelled to play the number for La Charada's chicken, number eleven, on the lottery.

Havana is neither the gambling place nor the Chinese place it was in Greene's day, but La Charada is not forgotten. In contemporary Havana slang, Fidel Castro is known as El Caballo, the horse. One of the easier Cuban sobriquets to explain, it comes from the horse on the top of El Chino's head. More difficult to explain is why Habaneros call Raúl—Fidel's brother, now the president—La China, which is a Chinese woman.

·

SINCE COMMUNISM ESPOUSES state ownership, it can be seen as an experiment in the limits of government. Whether in Russia, Hungary, China, or Cuba, it was always evident that the government was good at providing education and health care and very bad at running restaurants.

In Havana after the revolution, the state started some new restaurants, including a Bulgarian and a Russian one. It also tried to keep open some iconic places, including the Tropicana nightclub, Sloppy Joe's, El Floridita, and La Bodeguita del Medio. Sloppy Joe's was lost in 1965—because of a fire, according to some, or because of the bureaucracy of the nationalization program, according to others. El Floridita remained open except for a brief period of renovation, and La Bodeguita never closed.

Sloppy Joe's was reopened in 2013 by a Cuban government agency that has been restoring the historic houses in nearby Habana Vieja. This was an unusual experiment in socialist restaurateurship. They researched the site with old photographs and interviews and the same care with which they restored the Catedral de la Virgen María and historic mansions and government buildings. The restaurant was faithfully re-created, down to its menu and drinks, and now looks exactly as it did in the Carol Reed film—sleek and far from sloppy. It also once again serves its famous Sloppy Joes—the sandwich and the drink.

•

SLOPPY JOE'S, EL Floridita, and La Bodeguita were all known as Hemingway haunts, and that may explain their survival. Havana never passes up the opportunity for a Hemingway site.

Hemingway is remembered wherever he spent time—Oak Park (Illinois), Paris, Madrid, Key West, and Ketchum (Idaho)—but in Havana he is remembered with an obsession that borders on fetish. Only here do you learn that he wore no underwear and farted constantly. When Habaneros see any American of reasonable size with a white beard, they call out "Papa" to him. This has happened to me more than once.

Cubans who knew Hemingway made a living the rest of their lives selling interviews. Only a few elderly Cubans with connections to Hemingway too vague to charge money for are left. Still, they are hauled out to display to visiting scholars and tourists, like artifacts of a bygone era. In Cojímar there is Ova, Osvaldo Carnero, who went with Hemingway to Peru to shoot the film versim of *The Old Man and the Sea* and caught a 1,539-pound marlin in a struggle that was filmed for the movie. He is brought out for group visits to Cojímar, along with a younger man who as a boy witnessed the shooting of the film and says he saw Hemingway on the set. And Cayuco, a small, wiry elderly man, whose real name is Oscar Blas Fernández, is available to visiting groups in Havana. He grew up near Hemingway's house and played baseball with his sons. Hemingway, he says, called him Cayuco Jonronero—the home run hitter. "Why?" I asked. "Did you hit a lot of home runs?"

"No," he answered, with a sheepish grin. "Only once."

Books about Hemingway are constantly released in Havana and are always top sellers, despite the fact that, due to a copyright dispute, Hemingway's works are generally not available in Cuba and few Cubans have read them.

Hemingway lived in Havana for three decades, longer than anywhere else, although he was constantly traveling and wrote very little about the city. His well-preserved home on a suburban hill has almost nothing of Cuba in it.

His house has become a museum and is one of Havana's most popular tourist sites. In 2015, the director of that museum, Ada Rosa Alfonso Rosales, told me, "Here in Cuba the word 'Hemingway' is magical. If I need anything from anyone, I say I am the director of the Museo Hemingway, and as soon as I say 'Hemingway,' the door is open."

The story of that museum sheds light on the Cuban Revolution. According to Rene Villarreal, the neighborhood kid who became the head of the household staff at the author's home, Castro unexpectedly showed up at the house after Hemingway killed himself in Ketchum, Idaho, in the summer of 1961. Castro, like most Cubans, was a Hemingway fan. A famous photo shows the two men at a Hemingway-sponsored fishing tournament in Cuba in May 1960, which Castro won. In addition to displaying the most ego ever squeezed into a single picture frame, the young Castro reveals by the look in his eyes that he is thrilled to be in the presence of the aging writer. That was the first and last time they met.

When the Comandante visited the house, Villarreal seemed so unimpressed by his presence that Castro smiled and asked, "You know who I am?" The young man, who by then was accustomed to dealing with celebrities, did of course know. Castro told Villarreal that he wanted him to stay in charge of the house, to keep everything the way it was and to give tours.

But the revolution was young and in the process of creating a bureaucracy, and soon Villarreal was complaining of government officials and military personnel changing things and destroying the house. They did not trust this man who had not been part of the revolution, was not a member of the Communist Party, and seemed to have little interest in the new order. Before long he was working on a sugar plantation, which the government required him to do before granting him an exit visa. Villarreal lived the rest of his life in New Jersey. After he died, in

2014, the Cuban state, through the Museo Hemingway, paid tribute to him.

In Habana Vieja, room 511 on the fifth floor of the Hotel Ambos Mundos is never rented. A guide waits there to take your two pesos and show you around the tiny room. When Hemingway first stayed there, in 1928, the hotel was new and had a handsome, high-ceilinged lobby with, of course, a fine long bar.

The walls of the lobby are now covered with Hemingway photos. Oddly, most are not from Cuba, and none are from the hotel. One is a blown-up photograph of Hemingway's signature, hung on the wall as if he signed the Ambos Mundos.

The hotel's original, somewhat scary cage elevator is still operated by a staff elevator man, who takes visitors up to room 511, located down a hall. It has a single bed in a narrow alcove. Hemingway always asked for this room except when he was with his wife, Pauline Pfeiffer, because, despite its small size, it had the best view in the hotel, looking out on Havana Harbor. No matter where in the world he was—the Gritti Palace in Venice, the Ritz in Paris, the Sun Valley Lodge in Ketchum—Hemingway always got the best room.

The view today is not as good as it used to be, because Batista—who would have ruined the city had he stayed in power—tore down a low-lying seventeenth-century stone monastery in front of the hotel and replaced it with a three-story steel-and-glass building, one of the ugliest in Habana

Vieja, blocking the view. That building was just one more reason for Hemingway to hate the dictator whose men had beaten his dog to death, not to mention several of his friends. But of course, by the time Batista constructed the building, in the 1950s, Hemingway was already living in his house on the hill.

Not everyone in Havana is enthralled with the Hemingway legacy. The sentiment of the restaurant owner in Madrid who put up a sign reading, AQUÍ NUNCA COMIÓ HEMINGWAY—"Hemingway never ate here"—is sometimes found in Havana as well. In one of the best scenes in Desnoes's *Inconsolable Memories*, the central character takes his girlfriend to the Hemingway house. When she spies Hemingway's enormous shoes, he explains knowingly, "Americans have huge feet. I've always noticed it, even the most beautiful women." This is a reference to another example of Habanero slang: foreigners—first the Spanish and then the Americans—are sometimes called *patones*, because they supposedly have big *patas*, or feet.

Leonardo Padura once confessed to harboring "a fierce love-hate relationship for years" with the deceased author. He described the museum that was Hemingway's house as "a stage-set devised in life to commemorate death." Novelist Abilio Estévez, whose family went to the house several times a year when he was a child, said that it had the "funereal feel" of all museums.

I find visiting there just the opposite: voyeuristic. You prowl around a man's house while he is away, as though he might be coming back. Havana tries to perpetuate this sense that Hemingway is still alive. In 2015, I overheard Italian tourists ask the guide in room 511 where the author was. They seemed very upset to learn of his death.

•

BY SOVIET TIMES, El Floridita was a state-run restaurant. No longer open to the street, it was sealed off with noisy, cold air conditioning pumped along the bar, even though energy was scarce. By then, too, it was no longer crowded.

When I visited El Floridita in the 1980s, there were still some bartenders who remembered serving Hemingway his sugarless daiquiris, which they offered as "a Papa." They had plenty of time to chat with me, because there were few customers. One bartender, Antonio Meilan, remembered the author as "a kind and affectionate man" who always ordered a double daiquiri with no sugar and only drank and never ate in the restaurant. But despite Meilan's memory, a number of Hemingway biographers do have the author hosting dinners in the back room.

At the time of my visit, the curved back dining room specialized in serving lobster, but rarely had guests. The lobster, *langosta*, a very large, clawless tropical shrimp caught off Cuba's southern coast, was a luxury, viewed by the government as a hard currency earner and thus strictly for foreigners. Restaurants for locals were not allowed to serve lobster. At El Floridita, the lobsters were served by waiters in tuxedoes, the last vestige of a different era.

At La Bodeguita del Medio, deeper into Habana Vieja, there were neither lobsters nor tuxedoes. Like El Floridita, La Bodeguita was supposed to be a Hemingway site, but by the time the writer was frequenting Havana, his taste ran more to the tuxedo crowd (though he was often slovenly dressed in a dirty guayabera and shorts), and it is questionable how much time he really spent here.

Amid all the messages written on the wall of La Bodeguita is a framed note in Hemingway's careful handwriting:

My mojito in La Bodeguita
My daiquiri in El Floridita.
— ERNEST HEMINGWAY

How drunk was he when he wrote that? Did he ever write it? The handwriting seems a little too perfect. When I first started going to La Bodeguita, even though it was by then a state-owned restaurant, Ángel Martínez, elderly and nearly blind, was still overseeing his old bodega. We never talked about the authenticity of the Hemingway note, but we did talk about Hemingway. Martínez was a Hemingway fan; he was, after all, a Cuban. He especially liked the author's Cuban novel, *The Old Man and the Sea*.

Martínez could quote whole passages of the book in Spanish. But about Hemingway at La Bodeguita he said, "I think he only came here three or four times. He went more to the Floridita. He came here, had a mojito, had a photo taken, and went to the Floridita to have more photos taken."

Hemingway didn't like mojitos because he didn't like sugar. At El Floridita he could get his daiquiris without sugar. This upsets Cubans, who think everything should have lots of sugar. Many have concluded that he must have been diabetic, but he was very open about his many ailments and never mentioned diabetes. He just didn't like sugar.

If you ask for a drink without sugar in Havana, the bartender will usually say, "It's not going to taste good." But thanks to Hemingway, no one objects to a sugarless daiquiri at El Floridita.

At La Bodeguita there is one celebrity endorsement on the wall that is probably authentic. Errol Flynn scribbled, BEST PLACE TO GET DRUNK. It's true.

•

GOVERNMENT-SPONSORED DINING AND good eating perfectly intersected at one point: ice cream. Fidel Castro loved ice cream. He was famous for interrupting long interviews and work sessions for "an ice cream break," and novelist Gabriel García Márquez wrote that he once "finished off a good-sized lunch with 18 scoops of ice-cream." And if the Cuban Revolution was providing the Cuban people with health care, literacy, education, and food rations, wasn't there also an obligation in this hot, muggy tropical city to provide the people with ice cream?

Castro delegated the project to Celia Sánchez, an early revolutionary in Oriente Province, where the uprising began. The first woman to organize a combat unit, she had chosen the landing site for Fidel's invasion and, after the leading cigar makers went into exile, created the Cohiba cigar that Fidel famously and stylishly smoked until 1985, when his doctors told him to quit. Always a close associate of Castro, it has frequently been suggested—this being Cuba—that they were lovers.

Sánchez was also a fan of ballet. She named the proposed ice cream shop Coppelia, after her favorite ballet. The logo is a pair of chubby legs in a tutu and pointe shoes. That's what happens to ballerinas who eat too much ice cream.

Coppelia was built on a prime Vedado spot in La Rampa, on a lot where a nineteenth-century hospital had been torn down under Batista in 1954 in order to build a modern fifty-story tower. The revolution scrapped that and many similar plans for Havana. Instead, the space became a public park. But by 1966 it was a very run-down place with a few dilapidated stalls in what was supposed to be a beer garden.

Castro wanted Coppelia built in time for an international conference, which meant it had to be completed in six months. The site was favored because important delegations to the conference, especially the Soviet delegation, were to be staying at the nearby Habana Libre.

For better or worse, most of the island's leading architects had gone into exile by then. The leaders of the revolution and the young architects they'd chosen were drawn to fifties modernism, an aesthetic that favored circles over boxes.

Architect Mario Girona designed a structure suited to Cuba's unique situation and Havana's tradition. Central to the design were columns—prefabricated columns that could be brought in and installed on the site—supporting a circular structure inevitably referred to as a "flying saucer." The building was entirely Cuban-made.

According to legend, Fidel Castro was in possession of excellent recipes for thirty-six flavors of ice cream. Some versions of the story have him with more and some with less. It is not known where these recipes came from, but given the times, it is usually assumed that they were confiscated. He sent technicians to Canada to learn how to make the flavors and bought top-of-the-line machines from Sweden and the Netherlands. He wanted to build the world's largest ice cream parlor with the world's best ice cream for "the world's best people."

Girona did build the world's largest ice cream parlor. Much of its thousand-person capacity is in seating under banyan trees along pathways leading to the building. The capacity is not excessive if you believed Coppelia's claims to serve 4,250 gallons of ice cream to 35,000 people a day.

The wait in line was between one and two hours, occasionally longer. That no one seemed to mind is an insight into Habanero character. Standing in line at Coppelia became one of the rites of Havana living. You could go with a group of friends or meet people while waiting. For foreigners it was a way to meet locals, and for locals it was a way to meet foreigners. Once you reached the head of the line, the wait was worth it.

Opened in 1966, Coppelia was built for the same reason that Tropi-Cola was developed: to replace something lost by the embargo. Before the revolution, ice cream in Cuba had been imported from large American companies. Castro's goal was to locally produce better ice cream in a greater variety of flavors than any American company.

The original 1966 menu listed twenty-six flavors, all of which were usually available. They are worth mentioning:

Almond, coconut, chocolate, walnut, peach, tutti-frutti, coffee, coconut with almonds, caramel, orange pineapple, pineapple glace, dairy ice cream, strawberry, strawberry and assorted fruits, banana, guava, vanilla, chocolate and assorted nuts, chocolate walnut, mint chocolate, malt chocolate, vanilla and chocolate chip, mint and chocolate chip, muscatel, malted cream, crème de vie.

Crème de vie is an eggnog-type drink served in Havana at Christmastime. Have the exiles who say that the revolution is drab ever tasted crème de vie ice cream?

NINE

The Mulata Returns

Nowadays, no one ever imitates the Russians in Cuba; we
have the right to make our own mistakes now.

— EDMUNDO DESNOES, "Donde me pongo" (1967)

I N HAVANA, OYÁ, Santería's African spirit of change and
new beginnings, continued to rule. In August 1990,
Castro made a speech in which he said that the Soviet
Union might be dissolving and that this would mean tremendous hardships, even hunger, for Cuba. But, he said,
Cuba would remain true to its ideals and get through what
he labeled "a special period in time of peace." In a democracy, few leaders would have dared to be this candid about
impending hard times, but Castro decided to give people
bad news in advance.

Castro had offered the worst-case scenario, but he had
not exaggerated. The Soviet Union, which had been spending about six billion dollars every year subsidizing the
Cuban economy, did collapse. Within a very short period,
Cuba lost most of its imports and most of its export earnings. The gross national product declined by more than
a third. The island lost most of its energy supply, which
had come from Soviet oil. The lack of fuel was particularly

critical in Havana, where droughts are compensated for by the costly pumping of underground water. Cars disappeared from the streets; there was nothing for the Chevys and Ladas to run on.

But, like a gift from Oyá, inexpensive Chinese bicycles started appearing all over Havana. And some entrepreneurs built carts—wagons filled with seats—to trail behind the bicycles and transport tourists. These long-railed bicycle rickshaws now filling the narrow streets of Habana Vieja resembled the old-time volantes.

There was also a lack of pharmaceuticals, which had come primarily from East Germany, and, as Castro predicted, there were food shortages. Food rations—a hallmark of revolutionary Cuba—were increased, but even so, the average person in Havana had a diminishing diet. Interestingly, like another gift from Oyá to this very medically conscious society, there was also a noticeable decline in heart attacks and diabetes.

The government looked for ways to rebuild the economy and get past the "special period," and Cuba decided, as all Caribbean countries eventually do, that tourism was part of the solution. Despite hard times, tourist sites like the Hemingway house were refurbished. (The house was repainted its original cream color instead of the bright white the young revolutionaries had chosen when they took possession.) The government encouraged foreign investments for the first time, though it still had to own at least 51 percent of an enterprise. Hotels were restored. Old mansions were converted into boutique hotels.

Even this very modest introduction of capitalism to the socialist system was a major adjustment for Habaneros. On the one hand, they were being offered an opportunity to improve their situation. On the other, they were being told that government programs were no longer sufficient to look after them. Novelist Pedro Juan Gutiérrez, one of the important chroniclers of this special period, wrote, "We had been locked up in a zoo for thirty-five years. We had been given a little food and medicine but had no idea what it was like out there beyond the bars. And all of a sudden came the switch to the jungle."

Possession of U.S. dollars, which had been illegal, was legalized. This greatly facilitated small-scale commerce with foreigners, such as with the bicycle taxis. It also infused a famously egalitarian society with an income disparity that often seemed to mock the ideals of the revolution. Almost any job in dollars paid considerably more than any job in pesos. The driver of a taxi could earn more than a college professor, a surgeon, a baseball star, or a top entertainer.

Of course, these being hard times and this being Havana, the new freedom greatly facilitated the reemergence of street scams, such as peddling second-rate "Havana" cigars for high prices, as well as prostitution. Once again, men waited outside the better hotels, ready to offer guests a choice mulata.

As this latter scene reveals, three ambitious goals of the revolution had failed: the elimination of the sex trade, the elimination of sexism, and the elimination of racism.

Revolutionary Cuba had guaranteed its people the rights to birth control, abortion, and divorce for the first time in the island's history; the Catholic Church was no longer in power. Vilma Espín, one of the original revolutionary combatants, married to Fidel's brother Raúl Castro, had taken on the issues of sexism and machismo as the leader of the Federation of Cuban Women and the driving force behind the 1975 Family Code, which wrote changes in marriage vows and women's rights into the legal system. The revolution boasted that it would create "the new man"; in the new marriage vows, grooms had to swear to help with the housework. And they do, but that doesn't mean that attitudes have completely changed. A government can eliminate job discrimination and give everyone access to medical assistance, but it is harder to change the way people think.

The status of Cuban women post-revolution is revealed in the evolution of Havana restaurants. In 1993, the possibility of legally operating a private restaurant in one's home—to be a small, simple, homespun affair—was proposed by the government. Even at the outset, this was an opportunity limited to a small number of people, because, given the nature of Havana housing, few families had apartments that would lend themselves to becoming restaurants.

These restaurants were called *paladares*—a word of uncertain origin. It seems to derive from the Spanish word for "palate," and as an adjective it means "tasty." It is often said to have come from the Brazilian soap opera *Vale Todo*, which aired on Cuban television in the early 1990s; the lead character had a chain of restaurants called Paladar. The name stuck, though the soap opera didn't.

A *paladar* served simple, traditional dishes—such as ajiaco, picadillo, and fried plantains in garlic sauce—in a small room, probably the former living room, set up with two or three simple tables, often of the folding, card-playing variety, while children curiously peered out at the customers from the kitchen.

Despite the new marriage vows, the cooking in these home *paladares* was almost always done by women. These home cooks did not necessarily project the image of housewives, however. In Habana Vieja, the cooking and hosting at La Mulata del Sabor was done by *la mulata* herself, Justina Sierra. Justina was a former actress of, as the French put it, a certain age, a woman a few sizes larger than the little dress with the plunging neckline that she usually wore while flirting with her male customers, telling them that cooking is "about love." But also, she was a very good cook.

New laws were passed in 2010 that allowed the *paladares* to become more sophisticated and ambitious. The kitchen was no longer in view, and children no longer stared out at the customers. The new *paladares* were housed in larger, better-decorated spaces, sometimes filling the ground floor of a Habana Vieja house or sprawling out into a courtyard. Clearly the definition of "inside a home" had been liberalized. And sometimes ambitions overreached. A *paladar* in Miramar, with an appealing tropical courtyard setting, served a dish garnished with a glass in which a goldfish was swimming. This posed an interesting question, both morally and gastronomically.

The definition of the *paladares'* home cooking, home service—all of it had changed. There were now waiters in black vests and white shirts. The housewife cook was vanishing, replaced by a chef-owner, who was usually a man and sometimes one trained professionally at the hotelier school in Havana. As the status and scale of *paladares* improved, women were gradually replaced by men.

•

THE NEW EATING establishments needed to buy fresh food, which takes some ingenuity in Havana. One source was Mercado 19 y B, named for its address in Vedado, which has long been frequented by members of diplomatic households. A well-kept, covered open-air market, it has limited choices, many dependent on the season: fragrant guavas in the winter, many kinds of plantains and bananas all year round, papayas, huge quantities of the juice oranges that used to be exported to the Soviet bloc in exchange for oil, some herbs and onions and garlic, and cachucha peppers, which are small and brilliant red, with only a hint of heat. There is also meat, but open-air markets are dangerous places in which to shop for meat in the tropics. A better choice is the frozen meat available in higher-priced stores in central Havana.

Another food source is the back seats of cars, whose owners drive around legally or illegally with produce to sell. It is impressive how many heads of cauliflower can fit into the back seat of a 1957 Chrysler.

In Miramar—home to well-kept embassies with well-trimmed gardens, and early-twentieth-century houses often art deco in style—fishermen sit by the sea with long poles catching *pargo*, which they will sell to restaurants. Sometimes they take orders in advance.

Only a few blocks beyond the large, well-groomed Spanish and Chinese embassies on Miramar's Fifth Avenue is a neighborhood called Atabey, where houses are more middle-class-looking but still well kept. Here, a man who is called Chino—a misnomer, since his real name is Rolando Oye and he is actually Japanese—has an organic farm. Oye worked as a helicopter mechanic until 1997, when he took up his father's trade. His father, who had been an organic farmer in Japan, immigrated to Cuba in 1935. Organic farming is easier than conventional farming in a country with a scarcity of chemical fertilizers.

Oye grows fragrant herbs—dill, parsley, mustard greens—bursting with tangy flavor, and tiny cherry tomatoes, plantains, and cachucha peppers. He uses his less-than-an-acre plot of land in the crowded capital economically, with brilliant planning, and enriches the soil of this hidden green space with natural compost. His tiny farm is a cooperative with 260 members. Nearby, his sister operates a similar cooperative organic farm.

One of the charms of Havana is that surprising little pockets of activity spring up in unexpected places. In a dilapidated and decaying city, Habaneros have a genius for finding ways of using overlooked or abandoned spaces.

On Calle Mercaderes in Habana Vieja is a restaurant called La Imprenta. It appears to be professional and well run, but it is set among ruins—the courtyard of a 1774 building. In 1905, a printer had set up a shop called La Habanera on the ground floor, but today the building is roofless and gutted, as are many Havana buildings. Partial walls and second-story stone archways are the restaurant's decor, along with tall, straight royal palms and other tropical plants. Habaneros are gardeners. They plant anywhere they have a space—on their balconies, in their apartments, in courtyards, in yards. Beautiful plants grow easily here and are a reminder that if people gave up gardening, lush tropics would overtake spaces very quickly.

Julio Garcia, a good-looking, burly black man, beefy in a city of lean men, is a waiter at La Imprenta, but he moonlights as a magazine food writer. This is not unusual. A by-product of a system that tries to provide everyone with a good education is that seemingly everyone has high ambitions. In April 1996, Castro commented, "Everybody wants to be an intellectual in this country. This is a vice created by the Revolution itself, by the universities."

Since the government opened up the possibility of earning dollars, however, Havana has also seen the reverse occurring, with professors and engineers eager to drive taxis.

Garcia describes the chicken stew at La Imprenta as an authentic peasant dish. "Real Cuban food is slave food. It is not European," he told me. And as with many popular dishes, this seems to be the case. Here is La Imprenta's recipe, in Garcia's words. (My comments are in parentheses.)

Kill the chicken.

Pluck it and clean it.

Chop it in pieces with the same machete used to kill it.

Put it in a pot with a little water (enough water to cover, adding four big pinches of salt, two bay leaves, and three large pieces of carrot), cook for a while (about seventy minutes) and remove bone (and skin).

Add small amount (one quarter cup) of oil, normal oil not olive oil (many Habaneros do use olive oil, usually Spanish, when available, though this is not the way of the true *guajiro*, the Cuban peasant) to a skillet, chopped onion (one onion thinly sliced is better than chopped) and garlic (five medium-size cloves, sliced). (Add onions and garlic to hot oil until wilted.) Add chicken meat and a lot of (two and a half cups of good, chunky) tomato sauce. (Add about a half-cup of the stock from the chicken pot.) Add salt (not necessary if stock is well salted) and black pepper (six good turns of mill). Cook for an hour or more, until you are ready to eat.

Garcia said that in the old days, they added potatoes also. But potatoes, which were never a staple crop in Cuba, are scarce in Havana. The state-owned farms stopped producing them, possibly because of low nutritional value; the government was very health-conscious. Instead you could add about seven disks of peeled yuca, sliced a third of an inch thick. You should have a pot of good chicken stock left over, and pureed black beans could simmer in this for fifteen minutes for a classic black bean soup, or you could simmer more pieces of yuca in the stock, then puree it and add milk and have yuca soup.

La Imprenta is only one of many new restaurants to appear in Havana in the twenty-first century. El Templete, not to be confused with a nearby monument of the same name, is a state-owned restaurant, but unlike earlier ones that relied on Russian restaurant expertise, it has developed with the input of Spaniards. The original manager of El Templete, in 2005, was a Basque who introduced traditional Basque dishes, such as peppers stuffed with salt cod and a fisherman's stew called marmitako. Then came a Catalan and then a Malagueño. With all these Iberian layers, the restaurant offers far better seafood fare than Habaneros have seen in a long time; seafood here used to mean either grilled lobster or badly fried *pargo*.

Before the revolution, affluent families would pass leisurely Sundays at the yacht club in Miramar or a beach house in Pinar del Río. On the way home they would stop off at a farm in the tobacco country west of Havana, by the hilly town of Guanajay, where there was a family restaurant called the Rancho Luna. The restaurant would take family photos, print them, and place them in cardboard frames that said RANCHO LUNA, for diners to take home as souvenirs. The restaurant closed in 1963, but the owners, the Garcias, stayed in Cuba and, with state financing, opened El Aljibe in Miramar on August 13, 1993, a waitress there told me—"That's Fidel's birthday," she added in a hushed, reverent voice.

A re-creation of its predecessor, El Aljibe has a thatched roof, tile floors, big tables, and stiff Spanish wood-and-leather chairs, and serves many of the old restaurant's favorites, like Pollo a lo Tinguaro, named after a sugar mill near Camagüey. This dish, chicken cooked with sour oranges, is a Havana staple.

The sour orange—*naranja agria*—is an orange-fleshed, green-skinned citrus fruit. Basic to Cuban cooking, they are hard to find elsewhere. A workable substitute is lemon juice mixed with orange juice. The trick is to create a taste like an orange but sour as a lemon.

Here is the Garcia recipe for Pollo a lo Tinguaro at El Aljibe (for four servings):

3 pounds of chicken
A pinch of salt

A pinch of ground black pepper
½ cup sour orange juice
½ cup flour
½ cup oil
5 thin slices of ham
1 slice bacon
1 slice long crusty Cuban bread (pan de flauta)
(The Garcias also use onions and garlic in their recipe, but they seem to have forgotten to list it under the
above ingredients. I suggest a sliced half onion and five
chopped garlic cloves.)
Cut up the chicken into eight pieces and season with
salt, pepper, and orange juice. Let it rest for a half hour
and then dust with flour. Fry (in the oil) the slices of
ham with bacon and fry separately the slice of bread.
Let them drain and run them through a grinder. Fry
the chicken in the same skillet and once it is golden, add
chopped garlic and onion. When it is almost done add
the ham-and-bacon mixture and finish.

•

IN THE PAST few decades, the Cubans have been rebuilding their tourist industry—without Americans. At what is
remembered as the height of Cuban tourism, the record
year of 1957, the island attracted 304,711 tourists. After
the revolution, when tourism was discouraged and there
were few visitors, that number dropped precipitously, to
only 8,400 in 1974. But in 1990, as the special period was
about to begin, the 1957 record was surpassed, and by 1994

there were 619,000 tourists. Even with only a few visiting Americans, and with the embargo still in place, Cuba, and especially Havana, has been seeing the largest number of tourists it has witnessed in its long history of tourism. Since 2010, Cuba has been hosting more than a million visitors a year.

Shops and boutiques, which had completely disappeared from Havana after the revolution, have opened again, often in traditional shopping areas like Calle Obispo. Here, the names of some of the fashionable shops from a bygone era still have their names spelled out in mosaic on the crumbling sidewalks in front of their old entrances.

Ceramics are back. This was a traditional Cuban craft, derived from Andalusian tilemaking. By the twentieth century, many types of objects were being made from ceramics, but after the revolution, ceramic making was stopped because of the tremendous amount of energy consumed by kilns. Yet in one of the contradictions that abound in this revolutionary society, summer programs for the children of good revolutionaries on the Isla de Juventud taught ceramic making. Those revolutionary youths have since grown up and are making ceramics—tiles, plates, and bowls with Cuban themes, and even statues embellished with political satire. One sculpture depicts Obama and Raúl Castro standing on the Cuban people.

Most of the new hotels are refurbished old hotels or large mansions turned into boutique hotels. In the mid-1990s, there was considerable controversy about the government financing the construction of a huge seventy-million-dollar hotel on the Malecón next to Meyer Lansky's dream high-rise hotel casino, the Habana Riviera. In twenty years, the government had gone from using a high-rise hotel as a dormitory for party followers to building a new one in the same neighborhood for tourists.

After having escaped the fate of other seaside cities blocked off from the ocean by its own wall of high-rise hotels, was Havana finally going to succumb? And why was money that was badly needed for restoration being diverted to such a project? The obvious reason is that the economy was counting on more tourists, and there were not enough hotel rooms for them. But revolutionary Cuba was supposed to be different, and such money-based pragmatism was, and still is, unpopular. So far, this avenue has not been greatly pursued, but the future is uncertain.

•

IN THE ONRUSH of tourism, what has happened to the old standbys? La Bodeguita del Medio is crowded every night with musicians playing the old songs, mostly boleros of love and heartache. Sometimes the group includes a *tresero*, who plays a uniquely Cuban instrument called the tres, a six-string guitar with three sets of double strings, often tuned in octaves. It was developed for that most Habanero musical form, the Afro-Cuban son.

Many in the crowd are young European males who have enjoyed too many mojitos and generally do not succeed in their pursuit of beautiful young Habaneras. Foreign men are unhinged by the way Habaneras do not look away when ogled. As Edmundo Desnoes wrote, "What is really extraordinary about Cuban women is that they always look you in the eyes: they never avoid being touched by your eyes or touching you with theirs." But this is often followed by a rejection delivered with a slightly ironic politeness that is also Habanero.

For centuries, foreign visitors have remarked on the unfailing politeness and warmth with which the people of Havana greet foreigners. They do not even exhibit hostility toward the Americans whose government tried for decades to starve them.

Over at El Floridita, there is a four-piece Cuban combo with maracas, also playing son. The band plays down at the end of the bar that has become a shrine to Hemingway, with photos, including the fishing one with Fidel, and a bust of the author. It looks like the kind of shrine to a chosen African spirit that you would find in a Havana home. If you were going to build a shrine to Hemingway, it would make sense to put it in a bar.

Standing at the bar where he liked to stand is a literally larger-than-life—but maybe he always appeared to be larger than life—bronze statue of Hemingway; he will forever be drinking at El Floridita. There are young people, beautiful of course, dancing, incredibly of course, to the music, and smoking. Fidel may have given up smoking in 1985, but hardly anyone else did. Papa, slightly larger than everyone else, is wearing the kind of stupid gee-I'm-so-happy-to-be-here smile you never see in any of his many photographs, not even the phony-looking ones. The young women are dancing around him, shaking their hips and completely ignoring him, and he is standing there looking at them with his silly smile. It is not a completely unbelievable scene.

At Coppelia there are still long lines, but the ice cream parlor is no longer an experience for foreigners. Cubans now pay in Cuban pesos, and foreigners in Cuban convertible pesos (CUCs). A CUC costs much more than a peso, which prevents foreigners from taking advantage of the extremely low peso prices and prevents tourism from making Cuba unaffordable for Cubans. But—and the Cuban government might not be unhappy about this—the two types of currencies have separated foreigners and locals. Coppelia now has a dedicated line for those paying in CUCs, and it has almost no wait time. Worse, although the menu on the wall for all customers still has slots for twenty-six flavors, only one or two or three have labels in them: strawberry, vanilla, and chocolate.

The revolution has lost its crème de vie.

TEN

The Sound of an African City

~~❧✦❧~~

Y bien, ahora os pregunto:
¿No veis estos tambores en mis ojos?

Well then, I ask you now:
Don't you see those drums in my eyes?

— Nicolás Guillén, "El Apellido" (1958)

THE OLD, FALLING-down houses of Havana can still
breathe because they still have no glass in their windows, only iron gratings. They no longer display lovely
young women like flowers, and novelist Abilio Estévez's
claim that you could peer in and see gorgeous naked bodies
as you walked around the city is, at the least, an exagger-
ation. But there is still probably no other city in the world
where a strolling visitor is afforded so many candid domes-
tic scenes. And what are Habanero families doing in their
homes? A lot of the time they are listening to music.

Walk down a street in Havana and you will hear music
coming from every window and doorway—boleros, son,
guajiras, danzón, conga, charanga, pachanga, nueva trova,
filin (proving that you don't need elevators for elevator
music), jazz, Afro-jazz, Afro-Latin jazz, rock, hip-hop.

Most bars and restaurants have live music, and most of the groups are good enough to make you stop and listen. Drums, maracas, and guitars, especially the tres, are traditional. Trumpets have always been popular, too, along with woodwinds. There are inexpensive clubs throughout the city, often housed, in the Havana style, in unlikely reused spaces; one such club, Fábrica de Arte Cubano, popularly known as la fabrica, is in a former brick factory in Vedado. The clubs have to be inexpensive or no one would be able to go. Some concert venues are even less formal—in vacant lots, or on the street.

Dance has always been central to Havana life. According to a Santería legend, told by Havana-born anthropologist Lydia Cabrera, Changó seduced Ochún by dancing. He started dancing and "she said 'yes' immediately, and they began living together." That is how it is supposed to work in Havana.

Trollope wrote, "They greatly love dancing, and have dances of their own and music of their own, which are peculiar, and difficult to a stranger. Their tunes are striking and very pretty." In *Cecilia Valdés*, life is centered around dances, and when the novel's young scion is assessing the white woman he doesn't love but is supposed to marry, he does point out in her favor that she is a good dancer.

Music never goes out of fashion, though dance styles sometimes change. The music of the revolution—nueva trova and pachanga—is still popular. Nueva trova derives from American protest music and was much popularized in Cuba by Joan Baez. Silvio Rodriguez and Pablo Milanés sang songs of the revolution and still do. Pachanga, which is still popular, is an upbeat blend of son and meringue, usually with the kind of satirical lyrics Habaneros love. It is percussion-driven dance music featuring bongos, congas, cowbells, and trumpets. Che Guevara famously called the revolution "*socialismo con pachanga*," socialism with pachanga.

But at the root of all Havana music and most Cuban music is son. It appears to have come from a mix of African drumming and Spanish songs. Though these two were first fused in Oriente Province, by 1910 son was the street music of black Havana, bongos and maracas marking its distinct and infectious beat. The use of the word "son" was by then already quite well established. The earliest mention of it is in a song called "Son de Ma Teodora," by a black Dominican named Teodora Ginés, which is thought to have been written in 1580.

African music, dancing, religion—any expressions of African culture—were feared by both local and foreign white people. In truth, they feared the black people who had been wronged—a fear that, as José Martí pointed out, was rooted in their own racism. A January 29, 1879 *Harper's Weekly* article on a black festival in Havana described the street dancing as "giving the beholder a feeling of being transported beyond all limits of civilization, into the country of gorillas and monkeys of all descriptions."

And so music was suppressed. When son first emerged in the streets of Havana, in the early twentieth century, it was shut down by the police, as were most forms of African culture. Son groups, *conjuntos*, caught playing on the street, as was the tradition, had their instruments confiscated. In 1919, soldiers in eastern Havana, in Guanabacoa, were arrested for immorality because they were dancing to son. But a rhythm cannot be banned. Son was unstoppably appealing. It took over Havana, and so it has remained. By the late 1920s *conjuntos* were gaining wide recognition, especially a group known as the Sexteto Habanero.

Son was played with a square bongo, maracas, vocals, and a *botijo*. The *botijo*, which also turned up on other Caribbean islands, was an earthenware jug with a hole at the top and a second off to the side, originally used to transport kerosene from Spain to the islands. In the nineteenth century, people turned them into musical instruments by filling them with water to various heights, depending on how deep a sound was desired. The jug was blown into, usually through the top hole, to provide deep vibrating notes. In the 1920s, son groups gradually replaced the *botijo* with a double bass. Both tres and guitar were added. The Sexteto Habanero added a cornet and became the Septeto Habanero. The group's players changed over the years, but it stayed together until its ninetieth-anniversary album in 2010.

Son spread with the growth of radio, which, like the railroad, the telegraph, film, and television, developed earlier in Cuba than in most of the world. By 1933 Cuba had sixty-two radio stations, most of them in Havana and backed by Americans; this was more than any country in Latin America had. The Americans who created these stations imagined them playing classical music, which had a following in Cuba, home to world-class musicians and composers. But popular music, especially son, took over the airwaves.

The rhythm of son consumed daily life in Havana. Street vendors, *pregoneros*, called out to customers with chants in the rhythm of son. These chants were then turned into a type of son songs known as *son pregón*. Moises Simons, a Cuban Basque, wrote a son that was the call of a peanut vendor, "El Manisero," peanut vendors being among the more popular of the many street vendors found in Havana.

In 1928, Columbia Records was the first to record "El Manisero," with Rita Montaner, and though there have been at least 160 recordings of it since, no one ever did it better that she did. She was also filmed performing it. *"Mani, mani, mani,"* she would sing out, holding the notes for a full four beats each while her upturned face showed an expression between pleading and ecstasy. Even if you didn't understand Spanish—and she had many fans who didn't—you would imagine from her voice and face that this song was about something far more emotional than selling peanuts. And then, in a rapid staccato voice, like the soft taps on a bongo skin, she would sing, *"Si te quieres por*

el pico divertir, cómprame un cucuruchito de mani. " "Peanuts,
peanuts, peanuts . . . If you want a little treat, buy from me
a little packet of peanuts." That was all, but she looked and
sounded as if she were in love, possibly with Havana.

A bigger hit was the 1930 Victor Records recording
of "El Manisero" with Don Azpiazú and his Havana
Casino Orchestra. The orchestra included Mario Bauzá
on the saxophone. Bauzá was an Habanero who went on
to create Afro-Cuban jazz, which changed the face of
New York jazz.

The Azpiazú recording was the first 78-rpm single of
Cuban music to sell more than a million copies. Apparently
the producers did not like the term *son pregón*, as it was
correctly labeled on the Havana sheet music, or even the
term "son"—they called the music "rhumba." This word
had not previously existed, unless it was a misspelling of
"rumba," a sensual dance between a man and a woman created by free blacks in Havana in the 1860s, from the threads
of memories of traditional African dance. Obviously this
is not what "El Manisero" is. But the word caught on, and
ever since, this typically Havana music has become known
throughout the world as rhumba, with few outside of Cuba
familiar with the real term, son.

•

A CUBAN ANTHROPOLOGIST once told me that if you listen
to an impatient Habanero tapping his fingers on a table or
countertop, invariably he will be tapping out son. I have

not been able to verify this, but what I have noticed is that people in Havana walk to son.

Anaïs Nin, a Parisian with a Cuban father, observed in her diary in 1922, when she was only nineteen and son was first gripping Havana, that Habaneras and Habaneros have a special way of walking:

> In the walk of the people about the streets is reflected a peculiar indolence. It is a slow dragging step, a deliberate swinging movement, a gliding, serpentlike motion . . .

If you happen to hear son on a Havana street, which happens quite often, look at the people walking by and see how perfectly in step they are.

•

THE PEOPLE OF Havana don't talk the way other Spanish speakers do. This is due to the influence of African languages. For a long time, most Cuban authorities on the subject denied the African nature of Havana dialect. That was because the intellectual class, which was mostly white, tended to treat African influences as merely unfortunate deviations in Cuban culture. Enthusiasts of white music, such as guajiras and criollas—country ballads in slow 6/8 time—they usually regarded the upbeat son as a degeneration of Cuban music. But then much of this thinking changed, mostly because of the work of a white Habanero, Fernando Ortiz.

Born in Havana in 1881, Ortiz founded the Cuban Academy of Language in 1926 and the Society of Afro-Cuban Studies in 1937. He wrote more than a dozen books, on everything from language to music to hurricanes. Ortiz insisted that Cuba was not Spanish or African or Taino, but a composite of all these groups struggling with one another to create a new culture. He called the process "transculturation." Transculturation, he wrote, was the result of a variety of cultures "torn from [their] native moorings, faced with the problem of disadjustment and readjustment of deculturation and acculturation." In this context, it became pointless to argue about what was or was not African. It was Cuban, and Cuban absorbs some African. To some today, this may not seem like a startling idea, but to Cubans of that time it represented a new way of looking at themselves.

Latin Americans generally speak differently than Spaniards. They abbreviate things. "Come here," *venga acá*, becomes *ven acá*, and "over there," *para allá*, becomes *p'allá* ("pie-ya"). In the Caribbean, *s*'s and *r*'s tend to disappear. *Como estás*, "How are you," becomes *Como'ta*. *Ustedes*, "they," becomes *utedi*.

The disappearance of *r*'s and *s*'s seems to be the influence of African languages. In Haitian Creole, which is a fusion of French and various African languages, there are few *r*'s or *s*'s. Where there is an *r* in French, there is often a *w* in Creole. *Gros*, meaning "big," is *gwo* in Creole.

While the dropping of *r*'s and *s*'s happens throughout Cuba, as well as in Puerto Rico and the Dominican

Republic, it is particularly strong in Havana. I have always liked the way Habaneros call me by my last name, pronouncing it "Koo-*lan*-key."

Foreigners, even from Spanish-speaking countries, are often frustrated by the way Spanish is spoken in Havana. They always were. In 1859, Richard Henry Dana wrote:

> I yield to no one in my admiration of Spanish as a spoken language . . . but I do not like it as spoken by the common people of Cuba, in the streets. Their voices and intonations are thin and eager, very rapid, too much in the lips, and withal, giving an impression of the passionate and the childish combined, and it strikes me that the tendency here is to enfeeble the language, and take from it the openness of the vowels and the strength of the harder consonants.

Much of this holds true today, although it is not clear whether Dana was referring to the speech of whites or blacks. At that time, the transculturation process was not yet complete, and whites and blacks spoke completely differently. This was the era of *Cecilia Valdés*, and in the novel, black speech is much more abbreviated than white speech. Blacks address a white woman as "*seña*," for *señora* and a white man as "*seño*," for *señor*. Those particular abbreviated terms have disappeared, possibly because they were associated with slavery.

Today, Habaneros of different backgrounds do not speak different dialects. They all speak a language infused with many influences, some of them clearly African. Ortiz identifies twelve hundred African terms commonly used in Cuban Spanish. The speech is just as rapid as Dana complained it was, with the words formed in the back of the throat and seem to roll down the tongue with growing speed and desperation until they finally slide out of the mouth, with many parts swallowed whole. Before a vowel, the *s* is dropped; it is replaced with an aspirated *h* so that *más o menos*, "more or less," is pronounced *máhomeno*. Some neighborhoods have their own accent, especially those known for their traditionally black culture, such as Cayo Hueso, in Centro Habana. Singer Celia Cruz had a Cayo Hueso accent, an accent with a cachet in Havana culture, just as a Brooklyn accent is the one for which New York is famous.

Every time Fidel Castro spoke, it was clear to everyone in Havana that he was not an Habanero. He spoke slowly, the syllables rolling rather than bouncing, with big breaks between phrases. This may have lacked cultural charm, but it was appreciated by foreign correspondents, even Spanish ones, because he was the one Cuban in Havana whom foreigners could understand.

•

LANGSTON HUGHES, THE Harlem Renaissance poet, had learned Spanish during his visits to his estranged father in Mexico. In 1930, he traveled to Cuba and wrote a letter to Jamaican Harlem Renaissance writer Claude McKay, very excited that he had found in Havana a young poet named Nicolás Guillén, who had "created a small sensation down there with his poems in Cuban Negro dialect with the rhythms of the native music." This was thrilling to Hughes because he had been writing black poetry in the rhythms of blues and jazz. Guillén had been writing in son. Hughes wanted to translate some of the work but found it difficult to find an English equivalent for the black slang and to keep to the rhythm of son. He strongly encouraged young Guillén to keep striving in the direction he was working. Soon after Hughes left, Guillén established a reputation as one of Cuba's most important poets with *Motivos de Son*, eight poems in the language of black Havana in the rhythm of son. García Lorca, traveling to Cuba in 1930, the year *Motivos de Son* was published, said that he was going to "the land of Nicolás Guillén."

Guillén shocked blacks and whites by writing about the African features of black people—hair, noses, and lips. He was a dedicated Communist, and his poetry was the music of protest—but, to paraphrase Che, protest with son:

> *Cuba, palmar vendido,*
> *sueño descuartizado,*
> *duro mapa de azúcar y de olvido . . .*

Two slow whole notes followed by rapid lines, like the son of the peanut vendor:

> *Cuba: sold-out palm grove,*
> *drawn and quartered dream,*
> *tough map of sugar and neglect . . .*

Hughes was right: Guillén is hard to translate, to put in another language and still keep it black, Habanero, and son. That is why he has never been as well known in other languages as in the Spanish-speaking world. In 1948, Hughes finally took on the task of publishing a small edition of a book of his translations of Guillén, avoiding the ones with the heaviest dialect. He substitutes Harlem slang for the slang of black Havana, but they are probably the best English translations of Guillén ever done. Here is Hughes's translation of that great Havana motif, sweat, in "Wash Woman":

> *Under the explosive sun*
> *of the bright noon-day*
> *washing,*
> *a black woman*
> *bites her song of mamey.*
>
> *Odor and sweat of the arm pits:*
> *and on the line of her singing,*
> *strung along,*
> *white clothes hang*
> *with her song.*

•

IF YOU ARE walking around Havana looking in windows and who can resist this in a city of open windows; you are likely to see—especially in neighborhoods like Cayo Hueso, Regla, and Guanabacoa, known for their black culture—a doll, placed on a prominent perch with a large, quality cigar and a glass of rum. Sometimes you will see an adult sharing a drink or a smoke with his doll. Often the best seat in the living room will be occupied by one or several dolls. Most any kind of doll will work—some large, some small, black, white, or Asian. One afternoon in Guanabacoa, instead of a doll I saw the only couch in the living room occupied by a large, yellow inflatable bear, smiling ridiculously at his Cohiba cigar.

There are some other curious things to notice around town: bright-colored flags over doorways and windows, men wearing beads of the same bright colors as the flags, a circle with crossed arrows drawn on a wall, filled paper bags placed in the deep crevices at the roots of silk-cotton trees or the bases of royal palms, where bananas are also left. An Habanero pouring from a bottle of rum often splashes a few drops on the ground.

In a perfect example of transculturation, the practices of several African religions have fused with those of Spanish Catholicism to create what might be the most widely practiced religion in secular Havana. The dolls represent the spirits of ancestors; the flags and beads display the favorite colors of various African spirits. The spirits all have favorite colors. A follower of Changó wears red and white beads and a follower of the wise Orula wears green and yellow. These beads are very commonly seen in Havana. The paper bags under the ceiba, the silk-cotton tree, hold offerings to African spirits, orishas. The splash of rum on the floor is an offering to an orisha.

The ceiba tree, the symbol of Havana, is sacred to both African and European worshippers. The Spanish believed the tree was blessed by the Virgin Mary, because it offered her shade. Africans took it as a substitute for the African baobab tree, which also has big roots with deep crevices. The bark is used in African religions for medicinal teas, and the leaves are used for magic potions such as love spells.

Offerings under the royal palm, the straight and tall symbol of Cuba, are made to the West African orisha, Changó, who lives in royal palms and likes the color red but is also fond of bananas. Changó is associated with lightning, and the tall palms sometimes act as lightning rods. When the top is blown off a palm, someone invariably says, "¡Changó!"

There are three popular African-derived religions in Havana. The circle with the two crossed arrows most commonly seen on walls in Cayo Hueso represents the "four cardinal points of the universe," as found in the Palo Monte religion, which comes from Central Africa. The most popular African religion in Havana is Santería, the Cuban version of Lucumí, which is the religion of the Yoruba who today live in Nigeria. In Africa, the Yoruba are thought to have one of the richest cultures. Palo Monte ceremonies take place at night and involve consuming large amounts of rum and beating large, deep drums, while Santería ceremonies are performed in daylight, with heavy drinking discouraged, and the drums small and two-sided, tapped in intricate rhythms.

There is a third popular African religion in Havana, Arará, which had a larger influence in Haiti. Arará was the religion of the kingdom of Dahomey, which was established in 1600 in what is today Benin and was dominated by the Fon people. It had been one of several strong independent West African states. The Yoruba had had another one. But Europeans eventually destroyed them all, Dahomey being defeated by the late nineteenth century.

In all three religions there is a God, but there are also many spirits, orishas, that have tremendous powers. God, known in Yoruba as Olodumare, is all-powerful, has always existed, and is largely incomprehensible. The orishas were created by God and have human failings such as anger, jealousy, and greed. Each orisha has his or her own personality. Unlike God, they are accessible, and can be appeased and even won over through offerings.

To truly connect with a spirit in any of these three religions, the worshipper must invite the spirit to possess his or her body through ritual dancing. The process is extraordinary to observe. As the spirit takes over, not only does the style of dancing change from the dancer's style to that of the spirit, but the facial expressions, gestures, voice, and entire personality of the worshipper are transformed as well. In many instances this transformation appears faked, but sometimes it seems as if some other force has taken over with a disturbing intensity, and it is very difficult to bring the worshipper back.

In Havana, many people—white, mixed, and black—practice all three of these religions and also Roman Catholicism, following an African attitude that all religions are useful and you employ whatever is best for the task at hand. Cuba is supposed to be a secular society, and in Havana this point is often made. But while Habaneros are not drawn to religious institutions, they seem very drawn to beliefs. In his novella *El Juego de la Viola* (*Leapfrog*), contemporary Habanero writer Guillermo Rosales wrote about a boy who starts to say, "I swear to God," and then realizes that it makes no sense, since he doesn't believe in God. His father suggests that he swear on Father Stalin. You have to swear on something.

When Desi Arnaz, a.k.a. Ricky Ricardo, sang "Babalú" with his big drum, few Americans—though every Cuban—understood that he was singing a song to the orisha Babalú Ayé, healer of the sick. His choice of a Palo Monte drum may have been based more on dramatic effect than religious preference.

In Havana, most everything is suspected of having hidden African meaning. In 1926, earth was dug up in a central Havana park to plant a silk-cotton tree to commemorate a Pan-American Conference. The meaning of that was much debated; some suggested that the earth was actually dug up for the Palo Monte spirit Sarabanda, for whom earth is gathered. And why is the statue of José Martí surrounded by exactly twenty-eight royal palms? Is Changó guarding Martí? Why twenty-eight? Numerology is very important, with each orisha having an assigned number.

In Cuba, African culture was perhaps better preserved than in other former slave-holding countries. In the seventeenth century, European slavers stirred up animosities between tribes or nations in Africa so that they would go to war, take prisoners, and sell those prisoners into slavery. In West Africa, the Fon of Dahomey went to war with the Yoruba, defeating them, and a huge number of Yoruba were sent to Cuba and other slave colonies.

In Cuba, slavers had the same idea: if the tribal identities among slaves were kept strong, they would attack one another and could not unite. So they established tribal organizations called cabildos. Tribal traditions and culture were suppressed everywhere else, but they were encouraged within the cabildos. The whites regarded them as organizations to help them divide and conquer the island's black population. But black people saw the cabildos as centers for the preservation of their culture—their language, music, and religion. These organizations particularly flourished in Havana, making the city a center for African culture. The Yoruba cabildo in Havana was particularly vibrant, and rather than try to suppress other ethnic groups, it fostered rebellion against the white establishment, most famously in the early-nineteenth-century Aponte uprising.

In addition to cabildos, there were the Abekuá, secret societies formed to preserve African culture. As the free population grew, these organizations tried to look out for the economic interests of their members. Abekuá were especially powerful among the large free black population of Havana and controlled certain fields of urban labor, such as dock work, as well as certain neighborhoods, such as Regla, where the docks were and where most dockworkers lived.

Until the revolution came to power, with its negative view of all religion, Catholicism ruled the island, and African religions, like most elements of African culture, were suppressed outside of the cabildos. Transculturation, which subsumed African practices within the framework of Catholicism, occurred easily, because Catholicism has much in common with African religion. Catholicism has a God with three manifestations—Father, Son, and Holy Ghost, since 1962 known as the Holy Spirit—and beneath this, a huge pantheon of spirits in the form of saints and various manifestations of the Virgin Mary. As in African religions, each of these has a distinct personality and interests. Saint Francis loves animals, Saint Lazarus heals the sick.

At the edge of Havana lies a pretty little eighteenth-century shrine to Saint Lazarus. Every day people go there with a bad leg, a heart condition, AIDS, or some other ailment and ask the saint to heal them. But since Babalú Ayé also heals the sick, an undetermined number at the shrine go there to beseech Babalú and not Lazarus.

In 1989, I visited the shrine and asked the mother superior, an elderly woman named Isabel Valdéz Perez, who had lived most of her life at the shrine, how she felt about its being used for African worship. She said, "They change the names of the saints—they call San Lazaro Babalú Ayé and Santa Barbara something else. It isn't Christian. Christianity is Christ and the sacraments. But they are good religious people. Because they believe so much in God. They sacrifice animals." Here she wrinkled her face as though she had just bitten into a lime. "But I can't say 'No, you can't do that.' Those necklaces aren't from God, but if they want to believe that with a necklace they can communicate with God, there is nothing bad in that. If you reject a man of God for different customs, what kind of Christianity is that?"

Actually, it is the kind of Christianity that the Catholic Church practiced before the revolution, when they had power. But they could never stop worshippers from secretly bringing their African beliefs to church.

Even in Santería ceremonies that don't include Catholic practices, the various orishas are represented by images of corresponding Catholic saints. In Cuba, Babalú Ayé looks like Lazarus, and Changó looks like Santa Barbara. Oggún, who likes the colors green and black, and looks after wars and—conveniently for war victims—also hospitals, looks like Saint Peter. Yemayá, one of the most important orisha, the symbol of womanhood and maternity and also the sea, who loves the colors blue and white, is also the Virgin of Regla. This manifestation of the Virgin Mary, who has always been black (as, of course, is Yemayá), began in fourth-century Spain. She is the patron saint of Regla, the tough and weathered community on the east side of Havana Bay.

Catholics rejoice that even under Communist rule, Catholicism still lives in Havana with the huge pilgrimage to the Virgin of Regla every September 7. This ignores the fact—no longer a secret—that many of the pilgrims are there to worship Yemayá.

Women in Regla often wear blue-and-white gowns for Yemayá, and men dress in white for Obatalá, who looks after fatherhood and is also Our Lady of Mercy, celebrated in a church across the harbor in Habana Vieja.

Whites in Cuba are frequently involved in African religions, as well as those of Europe. This transculturation works well in a society where few are purely European or purely white, and where it is increasingly difficult to say what anyone's ethnicity is. As Guillén wrote in 1931:

> *Vale más callarse, amigos,*
> *y no menear la cuestión;*
> *porque venimos de lejos,*
> *y andamos de dos en dos.*
>
> *It's better to keep quiet, friend,*
> *and not bring up the subject;*
> *since we all come from far away,*
> *and walk together two by two.*

•

THE PRIESTS OF Santería, babalawos, are highly respected members of their community. Even after the revolution eliminated all private enterprise, the fees they collected for ceremonies and other sessions—in the case of animal sacrifice, substantial fees—were overlooked by the government. An Habanero might save for a year or two to be able to pay for a ceremony.

Babalawos study for years and, in addition to having knowledge of the ancient religion, must be able to speak Yoruba, the language of the orishas. In the 1980s, I used to visit a babalawo in Guanabacoa who, although only in his seventies, had learned the religion and language from his African-born grandfather, a Yoruba who had been sold into slavery.

I also used to visit a babalawo in Cayo Hueso. "Cayo Hueso" means "bone key," and in this land where everything is suspected of having a secret African meaning, that is an intriguing name for a neighborhood celebrated for its practitioners of Palo Monte and Santería. But in fact the name comes from the nineteenth-century Key West Cubans who moved back to this neighborhood. Cubans call Key West "Cayo Hueso"—simply because *hueso* happens to sound like "west."

The babalawo lived with his wife in one of several three- and four-story buildings that looked as if they would blow over in the next hurricane. And indeed, in 1970 a government inspector had come and told the residents that their building was unsound and was being condemned, and that they were to be moved to newer housing. But the residents were never moved, and the building still stood. As I climbed the steep, narrow, tilting staircase, it was difficult not to think about the twenty years the residents had been waiting for a new building. I also noticed that, as in most Havana apartments, the building's ceilings were twenty feet high—good for cooling hot air, but dangerous for living beneath, as pieces of loosening plaster had a long way to go before crashing onto the floor.

But this babalawo has some privileges from the government. As with other African religion leaders, he was allowed to practice his business of offering ceremonies and advice for a price.

One hot summer day in 1989, we got into his toothless friend's 1941 Chevy. To have one of these confiscated American cars usually meant that you were in the government's good graces, but a '41 Chevy is not a '58 Buick. It was a true *cafetero*, belching and bubbling along, with a stick shift that could only claw out two forward gears.

We were headed for a farm in Havana, which was good, because I was certain that this Chevy would never make it to the countryside. This was a special farm; it provided sacrificial animals for babalawos. "Without sacrifice there is nothing," the babalawo told me, and I knew he was not talking about the same kind of sacrifice that the revolution kept asking for.

Ritual killing is not easy. A little brown head can easily be twisted off a dove, but killing a chicken is more complicated, and a goat really takes some practiced technique. Our destination, an urban farm in a small backyard, had chickens, doves, goats, even turtles—Changó likes turtles. I was happy to see that there were no dogs. Oggún likes dogs, and they are sacrificed in Nigeria, but Oggún has to understand that no matter how African these Habaneros may be, they love dogs too much. Still, the babalawo told me, there had been some "extreme cases" in Cuba.

The farm's owner, a tall man with long, white silken hair and a kindly face, said that the business had been in his family for seventy years. When I asked him if it was secret or if the government sanctioned it, he shrugged ambiguously.

You really never know what you will find in Havana.

ELEVEN

Frozen in the Tropics

*Es ciudad en sombras, hecha para la explotacíon de las
sombras . . .*

It is a city in shadows, made for the exploitation of the
shadows . . .

— ALEJO CARPENTIER, *La Ciudad de Las Columnas* (1970)

HAVANA, TO BE truthful, is a mess. The sidewalks are
cracked and broken, as are most of the streets. Walls
are blackened from too much sunlight, whitened from too
much salt air, and reddened like rust in places where there
is no metal. Then there are the various molds, mildews,
and other growths that flourish in warm tropical damp-
ness and come in a variety of colors. Where there is wood,
it is being eaten by termites that drill holes with seeming
randomness and leave little piles of sawdust behind. With
structures sagging on their sturdy columns, sunken roofs,
stained gargoyles, and cracked and blackened stone orna-
ments, Havana looks like the remnants of an ancient civilization in need of teams of archaeologists to sift through
the rubble to see what can be found.

Elegant, sweeping staircases have lost their banisters.
Some hang at odd angles and appear to have only days

left before they fall. Buildings are regularly condemned as unsafe—according to the government, fourteen thousand buildings are condemned every year. Squatters sometimes live in them anyway. There are buildings missing stairways, missing roofs, missing walls. The government estimates that 20 percent of the population lives in housing that has been deemed "precarious." It is a reality that is reflected in literature—most contemporary Havana fiction is about people living in or somehow using abandoned buildings.

The city loses buildings every day. Habaneros seek uses for whatever survives. Some houses have collapsed, and only their facades remain. Rather than tear them down, Habaneros look for ways to use them—as with the restaurant La Imprenta, set among ruins. There are few wrecking crews or removal projects. In the center of Regla is the elaborate facade of a nineteenth-century theater. The theater is gone, but the facade awaits someone to build something behind it.

One of the remarkable features of Havana architecture is its balconies, made *"de fragantes barandas de hierro, como flores extrañas, secas entre páginas"* (out of fragrant iron railings, like strange flowers dried between pages), as the twentieth-century Havana poet Eliseo Diego put it.

Havana balconies were meant to be beautiful spots from which to steal a little evening breeze and hang over to look down to the streets. But now the decorative masonry is black, the walls are peeling, and the colored panes of glass that once surrounded doorways and windows have mostly fallen out, leaving wooden geometric skeletons behind, with only an occasional deep blue or red triangle to remind one of what once was there.

Balconies almost always have plants on them, usually in pots but sometimes growing straight out of the stone floor and rising more than a story, as if the rotting building were becoming organic enough to support more life than just mold and lichens.

Havana balconies never had much room for people, but now they have even less. They almost always have a line of laundry drying, because in this electricity-deprived city, clothes dryers are rare. Then there are the bright plastic children's toys, a bicycle or two, a broken-down machine in mid-repair. Sometimes there is a small coop or two for raising chickens. In earlier times, the balconies often housed roosters bred for cockfights. Nineteenth-century railroad regulations stated: "The hand baggage of a gentleman shall consist of one hatbox, one satchel, and one fighting rooster." Today cages more likely contain chickens for eating.

There are electric wires draped over buildings, stretched from one building to another, flopping out the windows, drooping down to the balcony and back in another window, making the city look like a seated marionette with loose strings.

·

SINCE THE REVOLUTION, the government has embarked on only a handful of projects to provide more housing. A few charmless blocks epitomizing the socialist ideal of "worker housing" were built.

Regla is a beat-up area of one- and two-story houses, the older ones ancient, crumbling, and made of wood, and a few model Soviet-built workers' homes, concrete two-story apartment buildings for good party members. It also has an oil refinery whose bright flames curl into the tropical sky and can be seen as far away as Vedado. Regla has a reputation as a good Communist neighborhood. One of the few uprisings in Havana to overthrow Batista was in Regla.

Castro did not want the revolutionary government to favor Cuba's capital city in its budget allocations, and it is obvious that it didn't. The government openly accepts blame for the state of Havana. The capital was never its priority, and, as with all difficulties and failings in Cuba, there is also the embargo to blame. In 1990, Raida Mara Suárez Portal, an historic preservationist for the city of Havana, complained to me, "There is no paint in Cuba." Paint is among the foreign products that are difficult to obtain.

But if old photos are examined, such as those of Centro Habana taken by Walker Evans in the early 1930s, it is clear that the city was in bad repair in earlier eras as well. In 1939, Alejo Carpentier wrote, "Havana is a city of unfinished works, of the feeble, the asymmetrical, and the abandoned."

Walker Evans, 1932–33. Plaza de Vapor, a market area in Centro Habana since the nineteenth century, known for everything from chickens in the 1880s to prostitutes in the 1950s. Evans's photos show that even in the 1930s Havana was a crumbling old city. © Walker Evans Archive, the Metropolitan Museum of Art

Similar observations were also made long before the thirties. In 1859, Trollope wrote of Havana:

The streets are narrow, dirty, and foul. In this respect there is certainly much difference between those within and without the wall. The latter are wider, more airy, and less vile. But even in them there is nothing to justify the praises with which the Havana is generally mentioned in the West Indies.

Alexander von Humboldt, the early-nineteenth-century Prussian visitor, did not like Havana any better than Trollope did. He described it as muddy, filthy, and evil-smelling. One of the problems at that time was that two thousand horses and mules were living within the city.

In truth, the foreigner who admires Havana has generally been an inveterate slummer such as Graham Greene.

Havana today is a city of dilapidated, formerly state-of-the-art buildings, erected to a large degree at the whimsy of the wealthy—from the ornate mansions they built within the city walls, and then abandoned, to the newer homes they moved into on the Prado and in Centro Habana, and in turn abandoned, to the even newer homes in Vedado and Miramar, which they also fled—along with their country—after the revolution. There are now no more rich people to take over these homes. But this differs little from the situation in the past: always, when the rich have moved on, there has subsequently been no market for their old homes, as they were deserting a neighborhood nobody with money wanted to live in anymore.

After the rich left, the state redistributed their cars, homes, and valuables to "worthy revolutionaries." Though it has never been documented, this must have been an ideal opportunity for corruption. In *Paisaje de Otoño* (titled *Havana Black* in English), Leonardo Padura wrote of a corrupt official expropriator:

One could imagine that a part of those recycled riches, minimal no doubt but very valuable (say a Degas that never reappeared, a Greek amphora lost to an oblivious Mediterranean, a Roman bust lost to memory, or collection of Byzantine coins never again exchanged by merchant owners of every temple there ever was?), passed through his hands with the promise of a revolutionary redistribution that never happened . . .

Writer Reinaldo Arenas, best known for his book *Before Night Falls*, told the story of an aunt, considered a good revolutionary, who was awarded a house in Miramar. There were many abandoned luxury houses in the neighborhood, which had officially been declared "frozen," meaning nothing was to be touched until appropriate new owners could be found. But it was difficult to qualify for one of these homes, and so the neighborhood remained largely abandoned, and every night the aunt would raid the empty houses and steal whatever she liked.

The revolution intended to solve the Habaneros' housing problem, but for most people, wherever you happened to be living on January 1, 1959, was your new affordable home forever. The state took over the buildings and the rent became extremely low. If you happened to be renting a small room in someone's house, you now had a very inexpensive room, and if you were living in a house or a large apartment, you now had an inexpensive house or large apartment. People did not move. Without new construction, there was nowhere to move to, and their current homes cost them almost nothing. There was, and still is, also nowhere for children to move once they grow up, and so today, even married couples live with their parents.

In 2012, I accompanied Mariano Guas, the son of Batista's vice president, back to Havana for the first time since he was a schoolboy in 1960. He found everyone living exactly where he had left them. We visited his former home, a ground-floor apartment in Miramar. The same family still lived in the apartment above. We went to his family's vacation home on the coast of Pinar del Río, and the neighbors were still the same. A few houses had been replaced by a military base, which he could not enter, but an officer told him that down at the base was a plaque commemorating the fact that Comandante Fidel Castro had landed there in 1960.

Mariano knew that. His family had spent the summer of 1960 at their summer home, because there were too many political fights going on among friends at the Havana Yacht Club. Mariano fell out of a tree and broke his arm, so he could not go swimming with the other children. He spent his time wandering along the shoreline. One day a launch pulled up and a bearded giant of a man came ashore. It was Fidel Castro. Though there was no one else greeting him, he walked right past Mariano without saying a word. That was the commemorated landing.

•

THOUGH MANY OF Havana's oldest homes are now in extreme disrepair, other old buildings are being preserved. Since the revolution, the government has taken to restoring historic buildings. They began slowly, with Habana Vieja's Plaza de Armas in 1964. Then, in 1982, UNESCO designated Habana Vieja and its fortresses a World Heritage site and provided small amounts of money to help with the restoration of the Catedral, the Plaza de Armas, and some other historic sites. As tourism revenue in the city increases, however, it can afford more restoration projects—and has a financial incentive to do so. Still, most of Habana Vieja, the only neighborhood in Havana that has been restored, remains dilapidated, with many homes even lacking running water.

It also does not take long for new rot to set into a restored building. Even the cherished Hemingway house has peeling patches and rotten corners. The truth is that it is almost impossible to maintain a city in a tropical climate, which relentlessly composts everything and eats all human endeavor.

In 1984, the government declared that rent money could go toward the purchase price of a home; in time, everyone could own their own home. This led to efforts by some tenants, now prospective owners, to fix up their buildings. One neighborhood where this famously occurred was Cayo Hueso, the traditionally black neighborhood of Centro Habana, giving rise to the phrase "Cayo Hueso intervention." Castro, who had been hoping that such initiatives would occur, suggested that other neighborhoods take on a Cayo Hueso intervention. But once the tenants restored their buildings, they had to take responsibility for their maintenance, and they had no better ideas than the government about how to do so.

By the twenty-first century, many Habaneros had paid enough rent to own their homes, and FOR SALE signs went up. But there were rarely any buyers, and when there were, there were few places for the sellers to move to. So neighborhoods are still, in the language of the revolution, frozen.

TWELVE

Sunny Side Up

Puede ansiosa
La Muerte, pues, de pie en las hojas secas,
Esperarme a mi umbral con cada turbia
Tarde de otoño, y silenciosa puede
Irme tejiendo con helados copos
Mi manto funeral.

Death then,
Standing among the withered leaves,
Can eagerly await me at my doorway
Every murky autumn evening, and silently
Approach me, weaving with frozen flaxen threads
My funeral cloak.

— José Martí, "Canto de Otoño" (1882)

José Martí is everywhere in Havana. Actually he is everywhere in Cuba, if you count all the small white plaster busts at schools and public buildings. Most Cuban heroes get only one statue; Martí has many.

Sculptors have improved on his appearance—being attractive is important in Havana. It is, in the words of author Hernández Roberto Uría, "a vain city that bewitches." Everyone is expected to be good-looking.

The police are good-looking; even the drug-sniffing police dogs at the airport—well-groomed spaniels—are good-looking. The revolution was started by Hollywood-gorgeous men, starring the tall and broad-shouldered warrior Fidel, with Camilo Cienfuegos in the warm and lovable role usually reserved in Hollywood for Eddie Albert: "the best friend." Ernesto "Che" Guevara, the violent revolutionary, looked too exquisite to be anything but a movie star. Allen Ginsberg, a famous American poet who supported the revolution, was deported in 1965 for too much talk about drugs and homosexuality; the final blow was when he said what a lot of men and women were probably thinking: that he would like to have sex with Che.

But Martí, always the central character in the Habanero drama, was problematic. "The Apostle" was a frail, five-foot-tall man with a few thin strands desperately hanging on atop his receding hairline. Had he lived past age forty-two, those strands probably would have fallen out, too.

Writers and historians have gone to great lengths to assure Cuba that despite Martí's unimpressive appearance, women found him irresistible. It is often suggested that it was his poetry that did it. María Granados, the daughter of the ex-president of Guatemala, fell in love with him when he was in Guatemala in 1877, but he was already engaged to a Cuban, Carmen Zayas-Bazán, and married his betrothed. María then drowned, either committing suicide from heartbreak or by accident, and he wrote a poem to her, saying not that she had killed herself but that she "died of love."

Martí's statues don't resemble the man in photographs. In stone or bronze or plaster, the Apostle has a high forehead and a thick crop of flowing hair, crowning a lean and robust frame.

The best Martí statue, square-shouldered and thick-haired, was erected in 1905 by the first Cuban president, Tomás Estrada Palma, in the Parque Central. Carved in Carrara marble by the leading sculptor of the day, José Vilalta de Saavedra, it depicts Martí stepping forward amid the royal palms (which must mean something) in his habitual coat, carrying some sort of cape or overcoat and raising his right hand while pointing with his index finger. Based on the statue's location, there are two prevailing theories about it, both of which illustrate the sardonic Habanero sense of humor. The Apostle of Freedom, according to some, is stepping out of the Hotel Inglaterra, which is behind him, and hailing a taxi. According to others, he is walking toward El Floridita, which is in front of him, and ordering a daiquiri. Personally, I reject both of those theories. Clearly Martí, a known baseball aficionado, is making a point about the previous night's game to the men who are arguing baseball every morning in the park below him.

Fidel Castro may have had his own theory about the gesture, because he used it constantly from his podium in the Plaza de la Revolución, with another statue of Martí perched awkwardly behind him. In fact, the Comandante may have been trying in many ways to imitate the Apostle, who was famous for his oratory. Castro often paraphrased Martí or even lifted from him, though Fidel was clearly too large and hairy and possibly too long-winded to pass for a second Martí.

An even more robust statue of Martí is the bronze one near the Malecón, where the Apostle is shown protecting a child and glaring menacingly at a threat from across the sea. This statue was erected in the year 2000, during the controversy over an attempt by Cubans in the United States to keep a small child, Elián González, from returning to his father in Cuba.

The most spectacular statue of Martí, and the one that best expresses his image, is not in Havana, nor even in Cuba, but in New York City, the longtime home of the Apostle, on Central Park South at the head of the Avenue of the Americas, a designated spot for mounted Latin American heroes. Two other heroes are also there—a parading Simón Bolívar and a galloping General José de San Martín of Argentina—but the statue of Martí falling off his mount is far more impressive than the other two somewhat static equestrians. Well-dressed and unarmed, though more balding than in most statues (perhaps because the sculptor was neither a Cuban nor a man), Martí has just been fatally shot, and his charging horse is tumbling.

The statue is by American sculptress Anna Vaughn Hyatt Huntington, who completed it in 1959 at the age of eighty-two. Her last work; it was a gift of the new Cuban government to New York. Relations having taken a bad turn, however, it was not placed in its current spot until 1965; the liberator Bolívar was moved to the side to make room for the Apostle.

Though the real Martí was carrying a firearm and was probably not dressed in city clothes when he died, the statue captures that tragic moment. Death is unusually important to Cubans, and especially Habaneros.

•

HAVANA HAS THE most celebrated cemetery of any city in the world except Paris, with its Père Lachaise. The 140-acre Cementerio Cristóbal Colón, where one million people are buried, is in Vedado. It has little shade and few benches, here in the broiling Havana sun, but it has avenues of monuments, some by renowned sculptors such as José Vilalta de Saavedra, who carved the 1905 Martí statue. The mausoleum of Catalina Laso, a wealthy woman who moved to France to escape a sex scandal was designed by René Lalique, complete with a Lalique glass dome with a rose carved in it.

Like the living city, the cemetery has a few well-cared-for streets, especially the main avenue that runs straight from the gate, where a motto reads, PALE DEATH ENTERS THE PALACES OF KINGS AND THE CABINS OF THE POOR THE SAME. But the monuments of the cemetery are not all the same. The richer people have the larger ones on the main streets. And as in the rest of the city, many of the sites are crumbling. Havana has a long history of exiles, and exiles cannot care for family graves.

Among the million buried in Colón are General Máximo Gómez; writers Nicolás Guillén, Alejo Carpentier, José Lezama Lima, Dulce María Loynaz; photographer Alberto Korda; anthropologist Fernando Ortiz; film-maker Tomás Gutiérrez; drummer Chano Pozo and pianist Rubén González; and the great daiquiri mixer Constante Ribalaigua, who has a chapel at his tomb.

One grave is a double-three domino. It is the grave of Luisa V. Antonia, who lost an important domino match by misplaying a double-three tile and then died of a heart attack. Another tomb is marked with a large marble chess king. It is the grave of one of the all-time greatest chess champions, José Raúl Capablanca. Born in Havana in 1888, he started playing at the age of four and liked to play many simultaneous matches. Once, in the United States, he won 168 games in only ten sessions. Havana has long produced great chess players—the Spanish brought the game to Cuba in the fifteenth century and it never left. It was one of the few things Russians and Cubans had in common in the Soviet era.

Havana is better known for baseball, and many of the great players and managers have ended up in the Colón cemetery, including Dolf Luque, who between 1914 and 1935 played for the Boston Braves, Cincinnati Reds, and Brooklyn Dodgers. Cuban League manager Alberto Azoy and Cuban Baseball Hall of Fame first baseman Julián Castillo are also in Colón.

There are hijackers, too, including William Lee Brent, a wanted Black Panther who hijacked a plane to Cuba in 1969. In the late sixties, there were so many Americans hijacking planes to Cuba, most of them black nationalists, that the Cuban government maintained a wealthy exiled businessman's Havana mansion as "the hijacker house," home at times to some thirty-five hijackers. According to one, Michael Finney, there were at one time as many as sixty American hijackers, most of them black, in Cuba. The FBI estimate was even higher. Many took advantage of the free university education and ended up with good jobs. Finney, who died of cancer in 2005, became a journalist, which may explain how he always knew when I was in town. He liked to talk to another American who had lived through the sixties. He and other hijackers admitted that they sorely missed the society of black America.

One of the most visited spots at Colón is the simple tomb of Amelia Goyri de Adot, who died with her daughter in childbirth in 1901. The baby was buried at her feet, but two years later, when Goyri de Adot was disinterred for reburial, a common practice, the baby's remains were found in her arms. These things happen in Colón because the ground shifts, which is why the cemetery reburies after two years. But not everyone accepts that explanation, and pregnant women visit La Milagrosa, the miraculous one, as she is now known. When they leave, they back out of the avenue so as not to turn their back on her. Habaneros, for a secular people, have a lot of beliefs.

•

MARTÍ WAS OBSESSED with death. At the age of sixteen, he predicted that his life would be short. His most famous collection of poems, *Versos Sencillos*, states in the first stanza that these poems are being told by an honest man who wants to release all the poems within him before he dies. The poems are full of death. Because of this, the Spanish Fascist movement of the 1930s, the Falange, which was almost a death cult, turned to Martí even though he opposed right-wing beliefs and was anti-Spanish. The Falange slogan was the nonsensical cry "Long live death." Their anthem, "Cara al Sol," comes from Martí's *Versos Sencillos*:

> *¡Yo soy bueno, y como bueno*
> *Moriré de cara al sol!*
> *I am good, and so I shall die*
> *With my face to the sun!*

Some, including Guillermo Cabrera Infante, have gone so far as to suggest that Martí committed suicide by revealing himself to the sniper in the grass. Now that Cuba was engaged in what Martí hoped would be the final war for independence, or so the argument goes, what else could he do to continue contributing? He was forty-two—older than he ever thought he'd be—had no military skills, and was of little use in combat. But if he died in battle, his face to the sun, a martyr—that would inspire the cause.

Thirty years before, the Cuban national anthem, which is still the national anthem of Cuba today, had called for martyrs. "The Hymn of Bayamo," or "La Bayamesa," was written in 1868 by Perucho Figueredo, supposedly while still on horseback after the Spanish defeat at Bayamo, and it states, *"Que morir por la patria es vivir"* (To die for the motherland is to live).

An ineffective soldier, Martí became a powerful martyr. The revolution loves him. Its bitter opponents love him. Both Communists and Fascists quote him. The Spanish he bitterly opposed all his life admire him, as do the Americans he mistrusted. Only a martyr could do this.

·

MARTÍ WAS THE first in Cuba's long tradition of martyrs and suicides. In 1958, when writer Reinaldo Arenas was a fourteen-year-old in the rural town of Holguín, he decided that he and his friend Carlos should run away to the mountains and join Castro's guerillas. They could not be like the real guerrillas, *los barbudos*, so called for the beards they wore, because they were too young to have beards, but they could, in Arenas's words, "take part in some battle and lose our lives."

Arenas recalled a trial, soon after the revolution, of a group of air force officers accused of trying to bomb

Santiago. Fidel Castro himself was prosecuting, but the judge, himself a woolly-chinned *barbudo*, a member of the movement, could see that the officers were innocent and ruled in their favor. Then, having gone against the movement, he shot himself.

There were numerous suicides in the early years of the revolution. Olga Andreu, a woman who hosted clandestine readings of dissident writers, mostly writers who had applied to leave Cuba, jumped off her balcony without explanation one day. A revolutionary named Eddy Suñol, in charge of the many executions of "traitors" in his area for fifteen years after the revolution, put a bullet in his own head. Arenas wrote, "Suñol's death was just one more suicide in our political history, which is an endless history of suicides."

Arenas also had an economics professor named Juan Pérez de la Riva, an aristocrat who was the only one in his family who stayed to support the revolution. A romantic who was always unlucky in love, he was allowed to periodically visit his family in Paris and jumped off a bridge every time he went there. But he never succeeded in killing himself. Finally he fell in love with a woman who loved him in return, and they were happy. Now he wanted to live, but he got throat cancer and died. That is a perfect example of a Havana story.

In Havana, suicide is a respected alternative. It certainly did not damage Hemingway's standing in the city. Arenas wrote about the high rate of suicide among prisoners at the Morro. It was a means of escape. Slaves had also felt this way. If you ask an Habanero, "How are you?" a frequent answer will be "Still alive." A similar response is used almost everywhere in the Caribbean where there is a history of slavery. For slaves, death was ever present. It also meant resistance and escape, as there was the common belief that, once dead, a slave's spirit returned to Africa. The Tainos also resisted the Spanish with mass suicides.

Arenas, who used to tell many suicide stories, ended up killing himself in 1990. When he saw cats leaping off Havana balconies, he thought even the cats were attempting suicide, which probably says more about Arenas than about cats. He went into exile and contracted AIDS and decided to avoid an unpleasant death by killing himself. But first he wrote an autobiography, significantly titled *Before Night Falls*, which resembles Martí's *Versos Sencillos* in that it begins by telling the reader that he is about to die and wants to get the book out before he goes.

Another lost writer is Guillermo Rosales. A Havana native born in 1946, he wanted so desperately to leave Cuba in the 1970s that, according to Arenas, he conceived of a plot to disguise himself as Nicolás Guillén, who, as a supporter of the revolution, was free to travel. Eventually Rosales managed to get to Miami without a disguise. There, he lived an unhappy and marginal life in halfway houses in the 1980s, but he continued to write, often destroying his manuscripts if there was no interest in them after a short period. In 1993, he destroyed all his manuscripts and fired a handgun into the side of his head. He left behind two novellas and five short stories—brilliant work, just a tease, enough to hint at what we are missing. Isn't suicide on one level or another usually an act of aggression, a form of attack? Weren't the slaves right about that?

A number of Havana mayors have killed themselves. Wilfred Fernández, a loyal Machado supporter, was arrested in 1933 when Machado was overthrown; while imprisoned in La Cabaña, he shot himself in the head. Mayor Manuel Fernández Supervielle put a bullet in his head in 1947 over his failure to live up to a campaign promise to improve the city's water supply.

The most spectacular Havana suicide in anyone's memory was that of politician Eduardo Chibás, often called Eddy and sometimes called El Loco, because buried inside him was a kind of fervor that makes people wonder. He considered himself a "revolutionary," but then, so have most Cuban politicians. For two hundred years, "revolution" has been an overused word in Cuba. When Castro came to power, many were surprised to find that his earlier proclamations were true, that he really wanted a revolution.

What made Eddy Chibás an unusual politician was that he was so wealthy that he had no interest in stealing, so he didn't like politicians who did, which was most of them. He originally supported Dr. Ramón Grau, a physician from a wealthy tobacco family who replaced Machado. But by the 1940s, he and many others suspected Grau of corruption, and Chibás organized a movement against him called the Orthodox Party. Of course, Grau and Chibás both claimed that their party was the heir to Martí's "revolutionary" movement. Young Fidel Castro was an Ortodoxo.

Chibás ran against Grau's chosen successor, Carlos Prío Socarrás, but Chibás was too unattractive for Havana politics. Short, stumpy, and balding, with thick glasses, he lost. This was more than El Loco could bear, and he rented a radio station from which to broadcast hour-long Sunday afternoon diatribes against Prío. With his squeaky voice, he was not even attractive for radio. Nevertheless, in 1950 people started turning against Prío, and Chibás started to become popular.

Just when he was riding high, though, he made a mistake by railing against an alleged incident of corruption that seemed false—it seemed that Chibás had been misinformed. He started to lose all his credibility.

This being Havana, it was time to consider martyrdom for the cause. At the end of his next broadcast diatribe, on August 5, 1951, Chibas announced, "This is my last call," a declaration often mockingly repeated for months in the heartless humor of Havana. Then he took out a .32 caliber revolver and shot himself in the stomach, a slow and painful way to die. The final pronouncement, the shot fired, the body thumping onto the table by the microphone—it was all supposed to be a dramatic message for his listeners. Except that, as Cabrera Infante said, "being a true Cuban politician," Chibás had talked beyond his allotted time, and during the whole grand finale the station had cut to a coffee commercial. El Loco died of his wound a week later.

Arenas's grandfather had set up a radio with an antenna fastened to a bamboo pole, because he wanted to hear the Chibás Sunday broadcasts. On the afternoon of the final one, Arenas's great-grandmother was leaning into the radio, and just before the finale, lightning struck the antenna, traveled down the wire, and electrocuted her. At the funeral, Arenas's mother was in tears, and he went to comfort her. "I'm not crying because of my grandmother," she said, "but because of Chibás."

•

IN THIS CITY devoid of commercial advertising, a certain poster about death is everywhere. It is the Korda photograph of Che with the message SOCIALISM OR DEATH! This might strike a traveler who didn't know Havana as a little strange. Why not something positive about socialism and life? Why not "Long live socialism"? But the rhetoric of the revolution, just like the rhetoric of Martí and the independence movement, was all about death. Castro, like Martí, always promised death. "A revolution," he said, "is a struggle to the death between the future and the past." A struggle to the death does not seem like a great future unless you have an inordinate appreciation of death. In fact, the angry-eyed Korda portrait is about death. It was taken at a funeral on March 5, 1960, for victims of an anti-revolutionary saboteur who had bombed a freighter.

In the language of the revolution: "Men die. The party is immortal." Or the slogan that most reveals the revolution's roots in the language of slave uprisings: "We will drown ourselves in the sea before we consent to be anyone's slave."

It is fitting that while such pronouncements are being made from the José Martí platform at the Plaza de la Revolución, turkey vultures—*aura tiñosa* in Cuban Spanish—birds of death often circle overhead. It is as though nature was displaying a Cuban sense of humor. These birds are very large and ugly, but graceful in flight, as is evident as they loop over the Martí statue. Naturally, in Havana street humor there are many explanations for why the vultures are drawn to this spot, but few scientific ones.

Perhaps they just like statues. A few miles away, in Cojímar, the birds circle over a bust of Hemingway. The town of Cojímar looks a little roughed up, as do all Cuban towns, but its one pristine object is the concrete platform with stairs leading up to the ring of pillars surrounding the five-foot stone block with the green bronze bust of Hemingway. He wears the same silly grin that he has at El Floridita. It is poor form to speak badly of this large metal bust that lacks aesthetic appeal and doesn't even look much like Hemingway, because it was paid for by the meager earnings of local fishermen who gathered their metal fittings and propellers to melt down for this likeness of their hero. The fishermen like the statue, and so do the buzzards.

•

FROM THE OUTSET, the revolution seemed in search of martyrs. Fidel, Martí-like, often spoke of his own death, his readiness to die. In 1956 in Mexico, preparing to land in Cuba to begin the insurgency, he said, "In 1956 we will be free or we will be martyrs."

Fidel understood the political value of martyrdom. The first time the people in Havana started to notice him was when he leaped onto Eddy Chibás's grave at his burial in Colón cemetery and delivered a stirring speech. But unlike Martí and Chibás, Fidel envisioned living and being in power, and doing both for as long as possible. When he finally died at age ninety in 2016 he probably improved his stature, because in Havana a dead hero is worth much more than a decrepit elderly one, even if he was kept out of sight.

Many were killed by Batista's men—thousands according to Fidel—and plaques and monuments were erected to them. But none were large enough to be a Martí-size martyr, a martyr who could stand for the cause.

On October 28, 1959, a twin-engine Cessna airplane carrying Camilo Cienfuegos crashed at sea and was never recovered. Dead at age twenty-seven, not yet a year after

Castro took power, he might have been the martyr of the revolution. Everyone loved Camilo, who had the revolution's most seductive smile. But there were problems. The best friend/nice guy is not ideal martyr material. Also, no one knows how Cienfuegos died. The plane just disappeared. Naturally, some said that Fidel had him killed, but there is no real evidence for that. He was probably the best-liked revolutionary, and his death is remembered every October 28 with flowers tossed into the murderous sea. But a true martyr needs to die in a showdown.

Then there was Che, who was not the nice guy, but the pure revolutionary, the Robespierre of the Cuban Revolution. In France in 1792, when the Convention accused Robespierre, who would become the author of what was called the Reign of Terror, of allowing the French Revolution to become too bloody, with too many executions, Robespierre replied, "Do you want a revolution without a revolution?" That was Che's point of view as well.

Fidel Castro admired Robespierre and his Reign of Terror and even said, "We need many Robespierres in Cuba." He had one, but Che, always the revolutionary, grew restless running a government and directing a bank. He left to continue the revolution, first in the Congo and then in Bolivia, where the Bolivian army, along with the CIA, killed him. Now the revolution has its great martyr, the revolutionary who gave his life for revolution, killed by the CIA. Legend spread that his last words were "Shoot—you are only going to kill a

man." In some tellings, it is "Shoot, you coward . . ."
There is a good possibility that he never said any of
these words, in which case it would be interesting to
know who made them up, because they embody a very
specific personality: brave, militant, macho, and with
little regard for human life.

THIRTEEN

How to Argue in Havana

> But we can't lean only on poetic delirium. Let's seek support
> too in what we can call scientific delirium.
>
> — JOSÉ LEZAMA LIMA, *Paradiso* (1966)

H AVANA ALWAYS SEEMS to be in a state of delirium, and every Habanero seems to have his or her own form of it. Poet José Lezama Lima lived in a state of poetic delirium, which ran afoul of the Cuban government's carefully reasoned scientific delirium. Lezama's masterpiece of poetic delirium, *Paradiso*, infuriated the Cuban government, though they probably didn't understand it, since it is so dense and wandering that no one really understands it. All of Latin America hailed *Paradiso* as a work of genius except the Cuban government.

The book ignores all rules of plot and narrative, and takes flight in all directions. Julio Cortázar, the celebrated Argentine novelist and a great admirer of the book, wrote, "At times, reading *Paradiso*, one has the feeling that Lezama has come from another planet."

How could the Cuban government condemn a book that no one understands? Chalk it up to scientific delirium, the revolution's elaborately constructed set of rules and principles and correct ideals.

In Havana, sex is always a favorite subject, and the more explicit the better. Cabrera Infante wrote a short story about a man who had sex with a sea turtle, and no one batted an eye. But when Lezama wrote about men and men having sex (as well as men and women having sex; one detailed scene described a man having sex with a young woman and then with her young brother), it was considered perverted, and the government banned his work from being published.

Lezama, who refused to leave Havana, spent the rest of his life in a kind of internal exile, unpublished and without work. The popular poet Dulce María Loynaz had a similar fate. She was a very different kind of writer but they had both committed the sin of ignoring revolutionary delirium—they had their own.

Until recently, there was almost nothing less acceptable in Cuban society than homosexuality. In Havana, men were always ostentatiously male; a male friend was not a "buddy" or "dude," but a "*gallo*," a rooster. On the streets, the worst thing you could call a man was *maricón*, *pájaro*, *ganso*—there were, and are, dozens of pejoratives, as well as a whole other set of negative phrases for lesbians, most of them containing the word *tortilla*, meaning "scrambled eggs." Gays were sent to obligatory military service camps, where they were subjected to cruel and backward attempts to "cure" them with electric shock therapy.

Then, suddenly, in the 1990s, with the flexibility granted to an absolute dictatorship, the state completely reversed itself on the subject. Today, openly gay people can—not commonly, but sometimes—be seen in Havana at rock concerts or street parties. Homosexuality is also dealt with in books and films.

The strength of the Cuban police state is that it is difficult to know what will lead to trouble. The state accepts criticism. Desnoes's novels, Padura's mysteries, and Gutiérrez's films are full of criticism of the state. But when Lezama wrote about homosexuality, that was a different matter. And when Villarreal, the man who ran the Hemingway house, ran afoul of the government, it wasn't because he criticized the revolution, which might have been acceptable, but because he showed no interest in the subject at all. In Havana, what could be more suspicious than not having an opinion?

Foreign reporters have always been perplexed at how freely the people of Havana talk about political issues. But there is no police state that could keep Habaneros from talking, from expressing opinions, from joking and poking fun at authority. That is almost the definition of an Habanero. García Lorca called them *hablaneros*, from the verb *hablar*, "to talk."

In addition, the government is constantly changing the rules of the game—and it seems certain that it will continue to do so. But despite all the changes, Havana remains Havana.

Habaneros seem to understand their country's ever-changing rules, but they are confusing to a foreigner. One night I was walking down a dark and deserted street in Centro Habana, cautiously looking around. Since the embargo had cut off the use of U.S. credit cards, my pockets were stuffed with cash. My caution must have shown, because a tall, thin young Cuban walked up and said, "Don't worry. You are safe in Havana. There are two million people and one million of them are police." (Habaneros love to walk up to strangers and make this kind of declaration, usually with an element of ironic humor.)

The tall, thin young Cuban was only slightly exaggerating. The police are everywhere in Havana. The green-uniformed MININT, the internal security police, are tough-looking in that way that Cubans can look. But the regular gray-uniformed Havana police are, to be candid, the sexiest police force I have ever seen—beautiful young men and women in uniforms so perfectly molded to their forms that you wonder if they have their own tailors. These police seem to spend their days on the street in groups of two or three, always a mix of men and women together, just teasing and flirting with one another.

Foreign reporters get very excited when people refer to either of the Castro brothers by one of their numerous nicknames or indicate the bearded Fidel by stroking their chin, as though they wouldn't dare use their names. But of course Habaneros love nicknames and hand gestures. Habaneros flap their arms like a bird to say "I'm leaving." They don't hesitate to refer to Fidel or Raúl by name, and they love political humor. A popular joke is: The Revolution's three great success stories: health care, education, and sports. Its three great failures: breakfast, lunch, and dinner.

·

REVOLUTIONS ALWAYS INVOLVE a certain degree of delirium, but Castro's revolution was particularly delirious. It was not just about power changing hands or about politically remaking the government. The goal was to change everything—to change social relations, including the relationship between men and women, and to put an end to materialism. The revolutionaries wanted to change human nature and create "the new man." (Though the new society was supposed to be less sexist, the phrase was always "the new man.") The new man sneered at personal enrichment. The state looked after him or her, and he or she was dedicated to serving the society.

All of this change was thrilling. Edmundo Desnoes remembered the early years, the 1960s, as the most exciting time of his life:

The intensity. The destructive macho embrace of revolution. To see everything turned upside down is shattering, gave me a "rush," as the young here/there now refer to meaning. That has remained with me and makes everything taste trivial. The passion of revolution has spoilt consumer pleasures. I have only death to look forward to, as I crumple up and rot.

But then the special period came, and Pandora's box was opened. When the Cuban government lost its Soviet subsidies, it could no longer provide for everyone's material needs. Before, the revolution had essentially told people, "We will provide your food, your housing, your health care, and your education, and you will use your abilities to provide some service for this society that has provided everything for you." No one—not doctors or music stars or baseball players—was becoming affluent. But they were contributing. They felt part of a great experiment.

In 1990, about the time Castro had first used the phrase "special period," I talked to singer Pablo Milanés. He was one of the great stars of nueva trova ballads. He earned only a modest Cuban salary, like the rest of his countrymen, and when on tour, pulling in millions in hard currency for the state, he still earned only four hundred pesos a month for himself. I asked him if he ever thought of leaving Cuba and becoming wealthy like a few other Cuban musicians, such as trumpeter Arturo Sandoval, had done. He said, "We prefer to live in this kind of society. We have the possibility to do our art. It makes a lot of money, but that is not fundamental for us. If we cared about that, we would live in another country and be millionaires."

But when the special period arrived and Cubans were told that in order to have enough food to survive, they had to fend for themselves—open a *paladar*, start a shop, sell something on the street, drive a taxi for foreigners—everything changed. Because once people started thinking this way, their anti-materialism outlook, their sense of contributing to the society, began to fade.

Baseball players who had been content living on small salaries became increasingly discontented. They always play for their hometown team, and their family and neighbors always go to their games to cheer. For away games, their fans packed into trucks or buses and followed them. But now, an increasing number of players started to think that money was more important than this comfortable and supportive system, even if it meant playing for strangers in a strange land. When a Cuban defects to the United States and plays for the major leagues, he is for the first time in his life, with the possible exception of a few international games, playing in a stadium where there is no one he knows.

By the late 1990s even soccer players were defecting to the United States to play professionally, though this meant that during international tournaments they could no longer play for either the Cuban national team or the U.S. national team—a player is allowed to play for only one national team in his career. But still, they could make more money playing in the United States, and making money was now a recognized and respected goal.

Doctors, too, once the humble heroes of their neighborhood, began forgetting about how they had received a free education and began demanding what they saw as their right, as doctors, to be rich.

•

IS ANYONE MORE delirious than the anti-Castro exile? What drives them especially crazy is that Fidel Castro's revolution has lasted, providing Cuba with one of the longest periods of political stability in its history. That was completely unexpected. Those opposing Castro left for Miami thinking they would be back in a few years. Instead he died in bed at the age of ninety with his succession and the continuation of the revolution firmly established. I once asked the former Dominican Republic president Juan Bosch, who was Fidel's friend and who, despite winning a democratic election, had been able to hold power for only seven months, what he most admired about Fidel Castro. His answer: "The way he survives."

Castro regularly called his opponents in exile either rats or worms. That latter term—*gusanos* in Spanish—is further evidence that Castro wanted to be a long-living version of Martí. Martí had also used the term *gusanos* for his enemies—Cubans who supported the Spanish.

Using the term *gusano* for exiles has caught on in Havana, where many have *gusano* relatives, and it is often said without rancor. There are also *gusañeros*, a word that merges *gusano*, the worm, with *compañero*, the comrade. A *gusañero* is a Cuban who lives abroad but supports the revolution.

Some writers living in exile, such as Reinaldo Arenas and Heberto Padilla, rendered their work almost unreadable by their obsessive hatred of Castro. Arenas even blamed Castro when he contracted AIDS in Florida. Cabrera Infante, the son of a founder of the Communist Party of Cuba, who left in 1965 and became a dedicated Castro hater, at least maintained a Cuban sense of humor about it by coining the word "Castroenteritis."

Even Roberto González Echevarría, in his otherwise excellent history of Cuban baseball, *The Pride of Havana*, felt compelled to expend a great deal of energy proving that Castro was not a professional-caliber pitcher—as many of his supporters have claimed. Undoubtedly he wasn't. Is it important to prove? There is no record of Castro pitching in the Cuban League, which is often claimed by his supporters. González Echevarría took the trouble to go through sports records at the University of Havana when Castro was attending law school and found a November 1946 Law School vs Business school game in which an F. Castro pitched for Law and lost 5–4. Of course, the author conceded, there are a lot of Castros in Cuba and this might not be *the* F. Castro. The only other games with evidence that Fidel pitched were a pair of exhibition games the Revolutionaries played shortly after taking power with the team name Barbudos, the bearded ones. There are a lot of photos of him from those games. The angry exile triumphantly shows one of these photos in his baseball book and points out that the Commandante, in a windup, reveals his grip on the ball, thereby amateurishly tipping off the batter as to the type of pitch he is about to throw.

It is a particularly pointless argument because Castro freely admitted that all the stories about his baseball skills were myths and said he was better at basketball. The Castro side is equally excessive. Many Castro supporters claim that Castro was recruited as a pitcher by the New York Giants, a claim for which there is no evidence.

The dialogue in Havana is all about making the claim, not establishing the facts.

The Nocout

*Lo mataré. ¡Lo mataré! Lo juro por . . . (¿Por quién vou a
jurar?) No puedo jurar por Dios. No creo.*

I'll kill him. I'll kill him! I swear to . . . (to whom
would he swear?) I can't swear to God. I don't believe
in Him.

— GUILLERMO ROSALES, *El Juego de la Viola* (1994)

$$\rule{2cm}{0.4pt}$$

L IKE DELIRIUM, DANCE, irony, humor, and glassless windows, baseball is one of those Havana things that is
always there—something else to argue about, even though
in recent years, Cuban television has been showing more
international soccer matches than Major League Baseball
games. Havana children have put away their small balls
and sticks and taken to foot-dribbling large balls down the
street. This might even be intentional on the government's
part. Just as baseball was originally popularized as a way of
embracing America and rejecting Spain, Cubans may now
be turning back to soccer as a way of rejecting the United
States and embracing Europe. Europe, after all, has become
far more important to Cuba's economy than the United
States, both in terms of tourists and as a trade and business
partner. But for the time being, baseball, even with these

Soccer game in the street, Havana. © *2015 Elliott Erwitt/*
Magnum Photos

signs of its decline, remains the dominant sport. In fact,
if the U.S. embargo ended and Cubans could play in the
major leagues in the summer and the Cuban League in the
winter, the way it was done before the revolution, baseball
would probably experience a revival in both countries.

From the beginning, baseball meant far more in Cuba
than just baseball. In the 1860s, when baseball was just
starting in the United States, Cuban students studying there
brought it home and organized teams to play against the
crews of American ships. So originally it served as a way
to show defiance on the part of educated Cubans toward
American arrogance. But in one of the great examples of a

self-fulfilling prophecy, the Spanish banned the sport, out of suspicion that it was being used to rally the independence movement.

In truth, there was little connection between baseball and the independence movement at first, except that it was attracting the same people: American-educated, affluent young men. But the Spanish argued that the game was an excuse for these troublesome men to arm themselves with wooden clubs. They also saw it as an American incursion into what was supposed to be a zone of Spanish culture. On this last point they were right. And in fact, once the Spanish banned the sport, Cubans did start embracing it as an anti-Spanish statement.

A baseball team was formed by Cubans in Key West for the express purpose of raising money for Martí's movement. Soon Martí himself became a baseball fan. Baseball even had its own martyr, a young Habanero, Emilio Sabourín, who used baseball to raise money and support for the cause, until the Spanish arrested him and sent him to a prison on the North African Spanish enclave of Cueta, where he died of pneumonia in 1895 at the age of forty-five.

Cuban baseball has always been centered in Havana. Cubans always play for their hometown team, so Havana, with its larger population from which to choose players, always has the dominant teams. Originally there were only three teams—Matanzas and two Havana teams, Habana and Almendares. The first game in this three-team league is said to have been played in 1874 at the Palmar del Junco, a Matanzas field that still exists. Habana beat Matanzas, 51–9. It is likely that there were earlier games in Cuba as well, but of course the story of the first baseball game in the U.S. in Cooperstown, New York, is also a fabrication.

A number of Cubans played professional ball in the United States in the nineteenth century, starting with the Habanero Esteban Bellán, who was a big hitter in U.S. professional baseball in the late 1860s and '70s and also organized the Palmar del Junco game. From 1900 until the Cuban Revolution in 1959, seventy-one Cubans played in the major leagues. Many more would have done so had black players not been banned from the majors. Instead Cuban black players played in the Negro leagues.

Once the color line was dropped in 1946, numerous top Cuban players could play in the Cuban League in the winter and the majors in the summer. That ended with the Cuban Revolution and the American embargo, although a substantial number of Cuban players have played in the major leagues since the revolution. There would have been many more if the U.S. government did not force them to defect.

After the revolution, the government said that baseball was not a profession. Players were still paid, but they received very low salaries, like everyone else in Cuba. Teams were reformed and renamed. From the beginning, Havana has always maintained at least two teams, and though the names have changed several times, one has always had a blue uniform and one a red. Havana's two teams of the 1950s—the Almendares Alacranes (Scorpions), in blue, and the Habana Leones (Lions), in red—became the Industriales and the Metropolitanos, respectively.

The Industriales were so named because at the time there was a campaign to increase Cuban industry, or as González Echevarría liked to put it, "Che Guevara, minister of finance, had embarked on the harebrained plan of industri-alizing Cuba." Today the Industriales, who play in Cuba's largest stadium, the 5,500-seat Estadio Latinoamericano, are the island's most popular and winningest team.

·

HABANEROS, BOTH FANS and players, have a brainy but also a conservative approach to baseball. It is difficult to say whether they approach the game the way they do because Havana is a city with a long tradition of chess, or if their approach reflects the way they think, and that is why they are also good at chess. They are not drawn to the game's flashier aspects. That may be why base stealing is little appreciated—it's a show-off move. The big home run hitter, the showy player who wants to be the hero of the moment, is not liked by Havana fans. Yoenis Céspedes, a big-hitting Cuban outfielder for the eastern team, the Granma Alazanes, who defected in 2011, said that he was motivated to leave not by politics or even money, but because he felt that Cubans didn't appreciate him. He may also have been frustrated because he happened to have been born in a town whose team never makes it beyond the semifinals in the Cuban League, and there was no possibility for him to move to a different team.

Havana produces great ballplayers because they study the game—the timely, well-placed hit, the shift in positions, when to bunt and when to swing, and whether a batter is more likely to walk or strike out. Havana pitchers usually have more finesse than power—deceptive breaking balls, tremendous control, placing pitches on the very edge of the strike zone, and a deep understanding of which pitch to use for which moment. Cuban pitching has probably also been helped by the use of aluminum bats; because of the embargo, Cubans cannot afford to be replacing broken wooden bats. These metal sticks have more life in them when the ball makes contact, and they don't break when a fastball cuts in on their handle. So it has become more important for pitchers to prevent batters from making contact unless implementing a specific strategy, such as inducing a ground ball for a double play.

It is always exciting to go to a ball game, and a ball game in Havana is always the opening of a debate. One day as I was leaving my hotel on the Parque Central to head out to a game, a bellboy came up and whispered to me, "Want a woman?"

"No, thanks."

"She's a mulata." An attractive woman in the corner of the lobby started blowing me kisses.

"No. I'm going to the baseball game," I said.

The bellboy couldn't believe it. "A *mu-la-ta*," he repeated with feeling.

"But it's Industriales and Santiago," I countered with equal persuasion. Santiago and Industriales is a bit like the Cuban version of the Red Sox and the Yankees.

"Santiago. Really?"

"*Claro que sí*. Should be a great game."

"Who's pitching?"

"René Espín for Industriales," I said.

"He's not that good." These Havana fans were tough. He started explaining to me what Espín's weaknesses were and what approach he had to take to Santiago's lineup. As he was explaining all this, the mulata in the corner was growing increasingly irritated, but he didn't notice.

At a game at the Estadio Latinoamericano, that odd mix of barbarism and elegance that is Havana is always evident. Pleasant-looking women serve Cuban coffee, dark and so sweet it seems like syrup, in ingeniously folded pieces of paper that serve well as a cup. During the fifth-inning break, the women go out on the field and serve coffee to the umpires. For most of the rest of the game, though, people are shouting profanities at these same umpires. And that is why the coffee, the only snack available at the stadium, is a much better refreshment than the snack available at stadiums in provincial Cuba, where only *chupas* (lollipops) are served. It is unimpressive to be shouting "*¡Pendejo!*" and other expletives at the umpires while sucking on a lollipop.

Beneath the shouting is a steady murmur. It is the sound of fans discussing the strategy of the game. This discussion continues after the game is over, as they leave the stadium and as they board buses home. And it is continued the next morning by fans or fanatics—it's the same word in Spanish (*fanático*)—in the Parque Central, in a spot near the José Martí statue known as the *Esquina Caliente*, the hot corner. The term, when not referring to this particular spot, refers to third base: There is no time to reflect on strategy at third base. Some play must be made instantly. It is the hot corner of the diamond.

The topic on one particular morning was about the fifth inning of the Industriales game the night before. The fifth inning, two innings before a possible victory—is critical in Cuba the way the seventh inning is in a nine-inning major league game, because in Cuba, if a team is ahead by ten or more runs after the seventh inning, the game is ended. This is known as a *nocout*, a term borrowed from boxing.

No *nocout* was going to happen in this particular game, because the score was tied. There were runners on first and second and no outs. The batter hit a soft grounder in the infield, and the Industriales pitcher grabbed it and fired it to his second baseman to force out the runner from first base. The second baseman fired to first to get the batter, but this allowed the runner who was on second to come around and score the go-ahead run. This meant that the Industriales were now losing by one run. But there were now two outs and no one on base and it would be easy to get out of the inning. But whether this or throwing to third was the right move was the heated topic the next morning in the park.

"*Coño, carajo, pendejo,* you do not give up a run in a tie game in the fifth!"

"Listen, you *hijo de puta*! There would have been only one out and two men still on base." Index fingers were jabbing with the precision of dangerous weapons. Overhead, a marble Martí was making the identical gesture. Veins were bulging, sweat was beading, one man was turning red. If someone who did not understand Spanish were watching, he would have thought this was a political argument that was about to turn violent. The Industriales had quickly gotten the third out, scored two runs in the sixth inning, and won the game, but that wasn't the point. It was an argument about strategy. Later, everyone would drink small cups of dark coffee together.

That's just Havana—a city "*apasionado y febril como el amor de una mujer fea*" (as passionate and delirious as an ugly woman's love), as Dulce María Loynaz, one of Havana's best-loved women writers, once rudely described it. Ever since the Spanish started founding their various Havanas, change has been a part of the city's history, and it seems certain that Havana will face enormous changes, perhaps some of them very soon. But the things that make Havana Havana, the delirious, crumbling metropolis of black and white despite its faded tropical colors, seem certain to endure.

ACKNOWLEDGMENTS

MY FIRST THANK-you goes to the people of Havana who for almost thirty-five years showed me nothing but warmth, humor, and hospitality while my country was trying to starve them.

A long overdue thank-you to David Brown who I accompanied on research and who gave me a wealth of understanding about Afro-Cuban religions.

Thanks to my agent and friend, Charlotte Sheedy, and to George Gibson, one of the great publishers, and Nancy Miller, one of the great editors, who brought me this project. How fortunate I am to be working with such people.

Thanks to Marian Mass and Talia for their love and support, not to mention picture research.

GENERAL BIBLIOGRAPHY

Antolitia, Gloria. *Cuba: Dos Siglos de Musica*. Havana: Editorial Letras Cubanas, 1984.

Barclay, Juliet. *Havana: Portrait of a City*. London: Cassell, 1995.

Bjarkman, Peter C. *Baseball with a Latin Beat*. Jefferson, NC: McFarland, 1994.

———. *A History of Cuban Baseball 1864–2006*. Jefferson, NC: McFarland, 2007.

Brown, David H. *Santería Enthroned: Art, Ritual, and Innovation in an Afro-Cuban Religion*. Chicago: University of Chicago Press, 2003.

Carter, Thomas F. *The Quality of Home Runs*. Durham, NC, and London: Duke University Press, 2008.

Chomsky, Aviva, Barry Carr, and Pamela Maria Smorkaloff, eds. *The Cuba Reader: History, Culture, Politics*. Durham, NC, and London: Duke University Press, 2003.

Cluster, Dick, and Rafael Hernández. *The History of Havana*. New York: Palgrave Macmillan, 2006.

Cooke, Julia. *The Other Side of Paradise: Life in the New Cuba*. Berkeley, CA: Seal Press, 2014.

Díaz Ayala, Cristóbal. *Musica Cubana del Areyto a la Nueva Trova*. San Juan, Puerto Rico: Editorial Cubanacan, 1981.

Duharte Jiménez, Rafael. *El Negro en la Sociedad Colonial*. Santiago: Editorial Oriente, 1988.

Eire, Carlos. *Waiting for Snow in Havana: Confessions of a Cuban Boy.* New York: Free Press, 2003.

Estrada, Alfredo José. *Havana: Autobiography of a City.* New York and London: Palgrave MacMillan, 2007.

García, Alicia, and Sergio. *El Aljibe: Un Estilo Natural.* Havana: Editorial SI-Mar, 2004.

González Echevarría, Roberto. *The Pride of Havana: A History of Cuban Baseball.* New York and Oxford: Oxford University Press, 1999.

González-Wippler, Migene. *Santería: The Religion.* New York: Harmony, 1989.

Griffith, Cathryn. *Havana Revisited: An Architectural Heritage.* New York: W.W. Norton, 2010.

Hazard, Samuel. *Cuba with Pen and Pencil.* Hartford, CT: Hartford Publishing, 1871.

Hill, Robert T. *Cuba and Porto Rico: With the Other Islands of the West Indies.* New York: Century Company, 1899.

Humboldt, Alexander von. *The Island of Cuba.* New York: Derby and Jackson, 1856.

Jenkins, Gareth. *Havana in My Heart: 75 Years of Cuban Photography.* Chicago: Chicago Review Press, 2002.

Klein, Herbert S. *Slavery in the Americas: A Comparative Study of Virginia and Cuba.* Chicago: Elephant Paperbacks, 1967.

Kurlansky, Mark. *A Continent of Islands: Searching for the Caribbean Destiny.* Reading, MA: Addison-Wesley, 1992.

——. "Cuba Moves to Clean Up Havana Harbor," *Chicago Tribune.* February 23, 1986.

——. "Cuba, Si." *Mirabella.* January 1991.

——. "Field of Dreams." *Gourmet.* May 2003.

——. "Havana Homecoming." *Food & Wine.* November 2012.

——. "Havana's Historic Watering Holes." *International Herald Tribune.* 1985.

——. "In Cuba, 800 Jews without Rabbi, without Harassment." *Philadelphia Inquirer*. June 2, 1985.

——. "Man without a Country." *Progressive*. January 1986.

——. "No Escape from Cuba Haven for U.S. Fugitive." *Guardian*. July 8, 1985.

——. "The Big Squawk." *New Times*. August 23–29, 1989.

Llanes, Llilian. *Havana: Then and Now*. San Diego: Thunder Bay Press, 2004.

——. *The Houses of Old Cuba*. New York: Thames and Hudson, 2001.

Leal Spengler, Eusebio. *Para No Olvidar: Libro Premero*. Havana: Ediciones Boloña, 1999.

Lobo Montalvo, María Luisa. *Havana: History and Architecture of a Romantic City*. New York: Monacelli Press, 2009.

Martinez-Alier, Varena. *Marriage, Class and Colour in Nineteenth-Century Cuba: A Study of Racial Attitudes and Sexual Values in a Slave Society*. Ann Arbor: University of Michigan Press, 1989.

Miller, Tom. *Trading with the Enemy: A Yankee Travels through Castro's Cuba*. New York: Atheneum, 1992.

Moreno Fraginals, Manuel, ed. *Africa in Latin America: Essays on History, Culture and Socialization*. New York and Paris: Holmes & Meier, 1984.

——. *El Ingenio*, 3 vols. Havana: Editorial de Ciencias Sociales, 1978.

Moruzzi, Peter. *Havana: Before Castro When Cuba Was a Tropical Playground*. Salt Lake City, UT: Gibbs Smith, 2008.

Ortiz, Fernando. *Los Bailes y El Teatro de los Negros en el Folklore de Cuba*. Havana: Editorial Letras Cubanas, 1985.

——. *Contrapunteo Cubano del Tabaco y el Azucar*. Havana: Editorial de Ciencias Sociales, 1983.

——. *El Engaño de las Razas*. Havana: Editorial de Ciencias Sociales, 1975.

——. *Entre Cubanos: Psicología Tropical*. Havana: Editorial de Ciencias Sociales, 1987.

——. *El Huracán: Su Mitología y Sus Símbolos*. Mexico City: Fondo de la Cultura Económica, 1984.

——. *Los Negros Curros*. Havana: Editorial de Ciencias Sociales, 1986.

——. *Los Negros Esclavos*. Havana: Editorial de Ciencias Sociales, 1987.

Pérez Jr., Louis A. *On Becoming Cuban: Identity, Nationality & Culture*. Chapel Hill and London: University of North Carolina Press, 1999.

Rampersad, Arnold, and David Roessel, with Christa Fratantoro, eds. *Selected Letters of Langston Hughes*. New York: Alfred A. Knopf, 2015.

Roberts, W. Adolphe. *The Portrait of a City*. New York: Coward-McCann, 1953.

Ryan, Alan, ed. *The Reader's Companion to Cuba*. San Diego and New York: Harcourt Brace, 1997.

Salas y Quiroga, José Jacinto. *Viajes*. Havana: Editorial del Consejo Nacional de Cultura, 1964.

Scarpaci, Joseph L., Roberto Segre, and Mario Coyula. *Havana: Two Faces of the Antillean Metropolis*. Chapel Hill and London: University of North Carolina Press, 2002.

Tattlin, Isadora. *Cuba Diaries: An American Housewife in Havana*. Chapel Hill, NC: Algonquin, 2002.

Terry, T. Philip. *Terry's Guide to Cuba*. Boston: Houghton Mifflin, 1927.

Thomas, Hugh. *Cuba: The Pursuit of Freedom*. New York: Harper & Row, 1971.

——. *The Slave Trade: The Story of the Atlantic Slave Trade, 1440–1870*. New York: Simon & Schuster, 1997.

White, Trumbull. *Our New Possessions*. 1898.

Williams, Eric. *From Columbus to Castro: The History of the Caribbean, 1492–1969.* New York: Harper & Row, 1970.

Zanetti, Oscar, and Alejandro García. *Sugar and Railroads: A Cuban History, 1837–1959.* Translated by Franklin W. Knight and Mary Todd. Chapel Hill and London: University of North Carolina Press, 1998.

BIBLIOGRAPHY OF HABANERA LITERATURE

Arenas, Reinaldo. *Before Night Falls.* Translated by Dolores M. Koch. New York: Viking, 1992.

———. *Farewell to the Sea.* Translated by Andrew Hurley. New York: Viking, 1986.

Augier, Ángel. *Poesía de la Ciudad de La Habana.* Havana: Ediciones Boloña, 2001.

Benítez Rojo, Antonio. *A View from the Mangrove.* Amherst: University of Massachusetts Press, 1998.

———. *Mujer en Traje de Batalla.* Madrid: Grupo Santillana de Ediciones, 2001.

———. *The Repeating Island: The Caribbean and the Postmodern Perspective.* Translated by James Maraniss. Durham, NC: Duke University Press, 1996.

Bosch, Juan. *Cuba, La Isla Fascinante.* Santiago de Chile: Editorial Universitaria, 1955.

———. *De Cristóbal Colón a Fidel Castro: El Caribe Frontera Imperial.* Santo Domingo, Dominican Republic: Cuarto Edición Dominicano, 1883.

Bush, Peter, ed. *The Voice of the Turtle: An Anthology of Cuban Stories.* New York: Grove Press, 1997.

Cabrera Infante, Guillermo. *Mea Cuba.* Translated by Kenneth Hall. New York: Farrar, Straus and Giroux, 1994.

——. *Three Trapped Tigers*. New York: Avon, 1985.

Cabrera, Lydia. *Afro-Cuban Tales*. Translated by Alberto Kérnández-Chiroldes and Lauren Yoder. Lincoln: University of Nebraska Press, 2004.

Carpentier, Alejo. *La Ciudad de las Columnas*. Havana: Editorial Letras Cubanas, 1982. First published 1970.

——. *Guerra del Tiempo y Otros Relatos*. Havana: Editorial Letras Cubanas, 1987.

——. *The Harp and the Shadow*. Translated by Thomas and Carol Christensen. San Francisco: Mercury House, 1990.

——. *Music in Cuba*. Translated by Alan West-Durán. Minneapolis: University of Minnesota Press, 2001.

——. *Reasons of State*. Translated by Frances Partridge. New York: Alfred A. Knopf, 1976.

——. *The Chase*. Translated by Alfred MacAdam. New York: Farrar, Straus and Giroux, 1989.

Desnoes, Edmundo. *Inconsolable Memories: A Novel of Cuba Today*. London: Andre Deutsch, 1968. Originally published as *Memorias del Subdesarrollo* (Havana: Ediciones Union, 1965).

Diego, Eliseo. *En Sitio en Que Tan Bien Se Está*. Havana: Ediciones Boloña, 2005.

Estévez, Abilio. *Inventario Secreto de La Habana*. Barcelona: Tusquets Editores, 2005.

——. *Distant Palaces*. Translated by David Frye. New York: Arcade Publishing, 2002. Originally published as *Los Palacios Distantes* (Barcelona: Tusquets Editores, 2002).

García, Cristina, ed. *Cubanísimo! The Vintage Book of Contemporary Cuban Literature*. New York: Vintage Books, 2002.

Greene, Graham. *Our Man in Havana*. New York: Viking Press, 1958.

———. *Ways of Escape: An Autobiography*. New York: Simon & Schuster, 1980.

Guillén, Nicolás. *Cuba Libre: Poems by Nicolás Guillén.* Translated by Langston Hughes and Ben Frederic Carruthers. Los Angeles: Ward Ritchie Press, 1948.

———. *The Daily Daily*. Translated by Vera M. Kutzinski. Berkeley: University of California Press, 1989.

———. *Guillén: Man-Making Words*. Translated by Robert Márquez and Arthur McMurray. Amherst: University of Massachusetts Press, 1972.

———. *Obra Poética*. Havana: Editorial Letras Cubanas, 1985.

Gutiérrez, Pedro Juan. *Dirty Havana Trilogy: A Novel in Stories.* Translated by Natasha Wimmer. New York: Farrar, Straus and Giroux, 1998.

———. "Era un Hombre Decente." *La Gaceta de Cuba*. July–August 2014.

Iyer, Pico. *Cuba and the Night*. New York: Vintage, 1996.

Lezama Lima, José. *Paradiso*. Translated by Gregory Rabassa. Austin: University of Texas Press, 1988.

———. *Poesía Completa*. Havana: Instituto del Libro, 1970.

———. *Selections*. Edited by Ernesto Livan-Grossman. Berkeley: University of California Press, 2005.

Loynaz, Dulce María. *Against Heaven: Selected Poems: A Dual Language Edition*. Translated by James O'Connor. Manchester, UK: Carcanet, 2007.

Martí, José. *The America of José Martí*. Translated by Juan de Onis. New York: Noonday Press, 1953.

———. *Diarios*. Barcelona: Circulo de Lectores, 1997.

———. *Major Poems*. Translated by Elinor Randall. New York: Holmes & Meier, 1982.

———. *Periodismo Diverso*. Vol. 23 of *Obras Completas*. Havana: Editorial Nacional de Cuba, 1965.

——. *Poesia Completa*. Havana: Editorial Letras Cubanas, 1985.

——. *Selected Writings*. Translated by Esther Allen. New York: Penguin Classics, 2002.

Méndez Capote, Renée. *Memorias de una Cubanita Que Nació con el Siglo*. Barcelona: Argos Vergara, 1984.

Padilla, Heberto. *A Fountain, a House of Stone: Poems*. Bilingual edition. Translated by Alastair Reid and Alexander Coleman. New York: Farrar, Straus and Giroux, 1991.

——. *Heroes Are Grazing in My Garden*. Translated by Andrew Hurley. New York: Farrar, Straus and Giroux, 1984.

——. *Self-Portrait of the Other: A Memoir*. New York: Farrar, Straus and Giroux, 1990.

Padura Fuentes, Leonardo. *Adiós Hemingway*. Translated by John King. Edinburgh, UK: Canongate, 2005.

——. *Havana Black*. Translated by Peter Bush. London: Bitter Lemon Press, 2006. Originally published as *Paisaje de Otoño* (Barcelona: Tusquets Editores, 1998).

——. *Havana Blue*. Translated by Peter Bush. London: Bitter Lemon Press, 2006. Originally published as *Pasado Perfecto* (Barcelona: Tusquets Editores, 2000).

——. *Havana Gold*. Translated by Peter Bush. London: Bitter Lemon Press, 2008. Originally published as *Vientos de Cuaresma* (Barcelona: Tusquets Editores, 2001).

——. *Havana Red*. Translated by Peter Bush. London: Bitter Lemon Press, 2005. Originally published as *Máscaras* (Barcelona: Tusquets Editores, 1997).

Piñera, Virgilio. *René's Flesh*. Translated by Mark Schafer. Boston: Eridanos Press, 1989.

Pérez, Armando Cristóbal. *Explosión en Tallapiedra*. Havana: Editorial Capitán San Luis, 2014.

Rosales, Guillermo. *The Halfway House.* Translated by Anna Kushner. New York: New Directions, 2009.

———. *Leapfrog & Other Stories.* Translated by Anna Kushner. New York: New Directions, 2013. *Leapfrog* originally published as *El Juego de La Viola* (Miami: Ediciones Universal, 1994).

Rosshandler, Felicia. *Passing through Havana: A Novel of Wartime Girlhood in the Caribbean.* New York: St. Martin's, 1984.

Sarduy, Severo. *Cobra.* Translated by Suzanne Jill Levine. New York: E.P. Dutton, 1975.

Smorkaloff, Pamela Maria. *Cuban Writers on and off the Island.* New York: Twayne, 1999.

Villaverde, Cirilo. *Cecilia Valdés.* Translated by Helen Lane. Oxford: Oxford University Press, 2005. Originally published in Spanish in New York in 1882. Edition referred to here (Mexico City: Editorial Porrúa, 1995).

Yañez, Mirta, ed. *Cubana: Contemporary Fiction by Cuban Women.* Translated by Dick Cluster and Cindy Schuster. Boston: Beacon Press, 1998.

———. *Havana Is a Really Big City and Other Short Stories.* Edited by Sara E. Cooper. Chico, CA: Cubanabooks, 2010.

———. *The Bleeding Wound/Sangra por la Herida.* Bilingual edition. Translated by Sara E. Cooper. Chico, CA: Cubanabooks, 2014.

INDEX

NOTE: Page numbers in *italics* indicate an illustration or photograph

A NOTE ON THE AUTHOR

MARK KURLANSKY is the *New York Times* bestselling author of *Cod*, *Salt*, *Paper*, *The Basque History of the World*, *1968*, *The Big Oyster*, and *International Night*, among many others. He received the 2007 Dayton Literary Peace Prize for *Nonviolence*, *Bon Appétit*'s Food Writer of the Year award in 2006, and the 1998 James Beard Award for Writing on Food and the 1999 Glenfiddich Award, both for *Cod*. *Salt* was a Los Angeles Times Book Prize finalist. He spent ten years as Caribbean correspondent for the *Chicago Tribune* and frequently writes books on the Caribbean, including *A Continent of Islands*, *The White Man in the Tree*, and *The Eastern Stars*. He lives in New York City.

www.markkurlansky.com